BLOODAXE ENGLISH POETS

JOHN OLDHAM

JOHN OLDHAM
Selected Poems

edited with an introduction by
KEN ROBINSON

BLOODAXE
BOOKS

ISBN: 0 906427 12 6

First published 1980 by
Bloodaxe Books
1 North Jesmond Avenue
Jesmond
Newcastle upon Tyne NE2 3JX

The publisher acknowledges the financial assistance
of Northern Arts

To the memory of P.U.

Printed in Great Britain by
The Bowering Press Ltd, Plymouth and London

Contents

Introduction

Although Oldham's work is little read and less discussed he is normally thought of as a satirist of great vigour and passionate intensity who was hampered by a poor ear for rhyme and rhythm. Had he lived longer he might have become more "correct": as Dryden put it, 'the harsh cadence of [his] rugged line' might have mellowed 'to the dull sweets of rhyme'.[1] This standard view is very much off-target: Oldham *chose* the rugged style of most of his satires: it was not imposed upon him by incapacity or carelessness. He himself was sensitive to the charge of roughness, defending his satires, in the preface to his second collection of verse, *Some New Pieces* (1681), on the grounds of decorum:

> I confess, I did not so much mind the cadence as the sense and expressiveness of my words, and therefore chose not those which were best disposed to placing themselves in rhyme but rather the most keen, and tuant, as being the most suitable to my argument. And certainly no one that pretends to distinguish the several colours of poetry would expect that Juvenal when he is lashing of vice and villainy should flow so smoothly as Ovid or Tibullus when they are describing amours and gallantries and have nothing to disturb and ruffle the evenness of their style.

The contents of *Some New Pieces*, which range from a caustic invective against a printer who had mangled the text of an Oldham poem, through the conversational ease of an imitation of Horace's satire I: ix, to the mellifluous movement of the English versions of two Greek odes, are witness to Oldham's ability to match his style to the 'argument' in hand. He included the versions of odes by Bion and Moschus to emphasise his versatility: he chose them as models 'which the greatest men of sense have allowed to be some of the softest and tenderest of all antiquity'. More than two and a half centuries later Ezra Pound was to be satisfied that the imitation of Moschus, 'bewailing the death of the Earl of Rochester', has a 'cantabile' quality;[2] and in Oldham's own time the range of his poetry did not pass unnoticed. In his elegy on Oldham's death, Thomas Andrews, for example, asked

> But oh! my friend, must we no more rehearse
> Thy equal numbers in thy pleasing verse?

In love how soft, in satire how severe?
In passion moving, and in rage austere!
Virgil in judgment, Ovid in delight,
An easy thought with a Meonian flight;
Horace in sweetness, Juvenal in rage,
And even Byblis must each heart engage![3]

The present selection should be evidence that Andrews' praise is not simply a gesture of friendship: the rendering of 'the easy and familiar way of writing which is peculiar to Horace in his epistles'[4] in the imitation of satire I:ix is not the work of a poet with a defective ear.

But the received account misses more important things than the range and variety of Oldham's work. Though he was especially given to satire, his work is also reflexive and self-critical. Oldham was a remarkably self-conscious artist for whom writing was heuristic. In his finest pieces he is so alert to the significance of his chosen form or mode that his work becomes a commentary upon it: he is not simply a satirist but a meta-satirist. To understand this quality of Oldham's mature art we must approach through the wider perspective of the work as a whole.

When Oldham was at Oxford, between 1670 and 1674,[5] he gained a reputation as a fine Latinist and as one 'given chiefly to addict himself to poetry, and other studies tending that way'. By the end of his Oxford years this addiction had prompted him to try his own hand as a poet; but it was not until 1677 that he was first published. On 4 November 1677 Lady Mary and William of Orange were married, and the following day Oldham composed a celebration of their union. Something of the attitudes and bearing of the early poetry can be gauged from this ode. There is little doubt that Oldham intended the poem as a bid for public recognition, but he was a fiercely independent man who would not compromise himself to win acclaim. He seems to have wanted to be known not only as a poet but as a passionately Protestant one, for the ode is a paeon to Protestant unity on the marriage of two Protestant interests and countries. It is a paeon, moreover, offered in the context of growing fears of a papist successor. Oldham composed it at the house of Sir Nicholas Carew of Beddington in Surrey. Carew, M.P. for Gatton, was one of the old Presbyterians who, as a modern historian puts it, 'were to be distinguished from the majority of the Whigs by a genuine and positive zeal for religious reform and Protestant unity'.[6] As if offering himself for caricature he would stand in the House and cry 'Cure Popery and you cure all'. Carew had already transmitted Oldham's work to the Court Wits through that other Protestant champion, George Villiers, Duke of Buckingham; and it was under Carew's aegis that Oldham entertained exclusionist sentiments in early drafts of his anti-papist *Satyrs upon the Jesuits*. It is not surprising that the poet should have adopted such a stance or that he should have found the house at Beddington sufficiently sympathetic to write there, for he himself came from a strongly Nonconformist family in Gloucestershire.

Oldham's grandfather had been as rabidly anti-papist as old Sir Nicholas Carew. As rector of Shipton Moyne near Tetbury in Gloucestershire, he fell foul of the Church authorities on several occasions, especially in the late 1630s and early 1640s when he was twice hauled before Laud's Court of High Commission to answer charges that he had preached 'erroneous doctrine'. From his Shipton pulpit he had inveighed against paintings in the Cathedral and against simony with a battle cry similar to Carew's: 'All things are to be bought and sold at Rome.' It was to be echoed by his grandson in the *Satyrs upon the Jesuits*. The grandfather's Presbyterianism is matched by the father's Nonconformity. Appointed to the rectory of Long Newton in Wiltshire, close to Shipton Moyne, under the Commonwealth, he was ejected in 1662 by the restored regime. He had been about nine years old when his own father had been most embroiled in dispute with the Laudian authorities: the poet was roughly the same age when his father was dispossessed. The Act of Uniformity forced many clergymen into 'taking to the plough or to manual occupations, others maintaining a precarious livelihood on little more than bread and water',[7] but by 1662 the Oldhams held sufficient estates at Shipton Moyne to be sure of a comfortable existence. The poet grew up in the atmosphere of a learned, materially secure, strict Nonconformist and probably slightly embittered home. When he went up to Oxford it was to St Edmund Hall, which in many ways offered him an extension of this atmosphere. Not only did the Principal, Thomas Tully (an ex-headmaster of Oldham's school at Tetbury), fill his hall with young men from the West Country, he was 'a person of severe morals, puritanically inclined and a strict Calvinist' who exercised a 'severe government' over his charges.[8] Even if Oldham discovered the worldly pleasures of wine, women and conviviality whilst at Oxford, he did so against the backdrop of familiar values. In the years immediately following Oxford his major contacts were predominantly sympathetic to his family outlook. After leaving University, he returned to Shipton where he addressed verses to members of local families, the Kingscotes and Estcourts. And once in his first teaching post, at Croydon, he forged a relationship not only with the true blue Protestant Sir Nicholas Carew, but with a local landowner and philanthropist, Harman Atwood, whom he treated in the elegy on his death as a paradigm of Puritan virtue. Just as Tully's regime at Oxford had given him a stable base from which to explore pleasures not available in Gloucestershire, so the support of Carew and Atwood at Croydon (especially Carew) balanced the temptations of the libertine thinking of Rochester and the Court Wits. Though Oldham was to remain on good terms with Rochester until his death in 1680, wherever there seems to be attraction to his life-style there is also criticism of it; and this equivocal attraction was succeeded by intense disgust at his susceptibility to 'the noise of a tumultuous debauch, or . . . stupefying wine'[9] as his background reasserted itself. In the years after Croydon the extensions of his home and upbringing are less obvious, but they leave their mark in a variety of ways throughout his work, not just in his zealous independence, anti-Normanism, and vigorous anti-papism, but also in his conception of honour, of freedom and of poetry as a vocation, and in the deep sense of man's sinfulness which feeds both his satire and his self-critical anxiety about the value of his work.

Oldham's adherence to the notion of vocation entailed a twofold moral imperative: he had first to ascertain where exactly his talents lay as a poet and then to use them to the full. The weight that Oldham attached to obeying these imperatives can be judged from the dismay that he felt when it seemed that he had been neglectful. In his meditation 'A Sunday thought in sickness' he complains:

> Ungrateful wretch! I've made my sins as numerous as those blessings and mercies the Almighty bounty has conferr'd upon me, to oblige and lead me to repentance. How have I abused and misemployed those parts and talents which might have rendered me serviceable to mankind, and repaid an interest of glory to their donor? . . .

Sorting himself out as a poet was central to his sorting himself out as a man. Indeed the clear analogies in the later seventeenth-century mind between the polarity of fancy and judgment with which he had to wrestle as a poet, and the polarities of passion and reason, faith and reason, and personal liberty and authority, meant that his work on his style went hand in hand with his moral, religious and political thinking. Critical self-awareness was an essential ingredient of success in the task which had been set for him: it is evident in every stage of his development.

The belief that by using his talents as a poet he could fulfil himself in relation to his God, coupled with a subjectivism which could easily attend the Puritan emphasis upon the personal apprehension of the Word, seems to have fuelled Oldham's early view of his poetry as inspired. Verse fragments of uncertain date in his autograph manuscript express this view:

> Am I deceived? or does my swelling breast
> Enlarge itself for some approaching guest?
> 'Tis so, 'tis surely so: I feel the ent'ring God
>   Within me shed his light and rays abroad:
> All vulgar thoughts and what was human found
> Are now in a diviner fury drowned: [10]

and it is expressed, too, through the pindaric form which he used for his earliest English poem, the elegy on his college friend Charles Morwent. Oldham was always alert to the implications of a form: he did not use the pindaric for the Morwent ode merely because it was fashionable or because it came to him through the major influence of his early work, his 'beloved Cowley'. Pindar was the very type of the inspired poet, and the pindaric style—which gave the fancy priority over the judgment —was an embodiment of inspiration. The French critic Rapin felt that Pindar's 'panegyrics are perpetual digressions, where rambling from his subject he carries the reader from fable to fable, from allusion to allusion, and from one chimera to another; for he has the most unbridled and irregular fancy in the world'.[11] Despite Rapin's thinly disguised dismay at Pindar's deviation from the correct, his description is fundamentally sound. Pindar's odes rely on the strength of his poetic personality and sense of occasion to fuse together apparently unrelated brief allusions. In the ode to Charles Morwent, a late metaphysical style provides a seventeenth-century equivalent for Pindar's allusive technique; and like that technique it relies essentially on imaginative assertion for the truth of its claims for its subject. But Rapin's suspicion of such subjectivity was to be felt too by Oldham who began to share his age's anxiety about claims to inspiration. He became haunted by the spectre of enthusiasm and wasted no opportunity to attack those who succumbed to it. From mid–1676 Oldham trained his sights on enthusiasm and enthusiasts: in parts of his imitation of Horace's *Art of Poetry* and his praise of Ben Jonson, in the 'Satyr against virtue' and the 'Dithyrambic', in 'The passion of Byblis' and 'The dream', and in 'Garnet's ghost', he portrayed critically those unbalanced by poetic fervour, by drinking and a self-centred thinking, by love, or by religious and political fanaticism. With these attacks came a more common-sensical attitude towards the poet's role; as Oldham put it in his imitation of Horace's *Art of Poetry*:

> Good sense must be the certain standard still
> To all that will pretend to writing well:

The transition from the early rhapsodic conception of the poet was not an easy one, for Oldham was aware of the extent to which he himself might seem to have been enthusiastic. Beneath its clear-sighted interest in the nature of wrong reasoning, the 'Satyr against virtue', for example, is reflexive. It takes the form of a self-evidently irrational monologue, supposed to be spoken by the arch-libertine, Rochester, in which Oldham uses the pindaric —once an embodiment of inspired imagination—as a symptom of unreason and libertinism. By implication the Satyr offers a critique of his own earlier style and stance. Oldham's second study of Rochester's libertinism, the 'Dithyrambic', is equally reflexive. Here inspiration, prized in a less empirical age as a "spiritual drunkenness", is reduced to actual drunkenness, and the pindaric is again preferred as an expression of befuddled reason. The distrust of the fancy which these studies of enthusiasm imply left Oldham with a profound fear that poetic composition itself might be fundamentally irrational and untrustworthy. The 'Letter addressed to a friend' expresses a tension between this fear and a belief that poetry was his vocation, his talent to employ in the service of his God. Viewed in one way poetry seems a 'disease', a 'distemper' and a 'wicked lust'; looked at from another angle it is something to delight in, and evidence of the poet's ability to give shape to unwieldy material. Even this more positive perspective is self-regarding. Whereas the poems attacking Rochester (and related pieces) had been implicitly reflexive as part of the dialectic of Oldham's development, the explicit self-criticism of the Letter marks the emergence of an important element of Oldham's mature poetic voice.

Despite his critique of the pindaric and disillusionment about inspiration, Oldham continued to write pindarics; but his movement away from the subjective towards the common-sensical and consensus entailed radical shifts of emphasis inimical to the spirit of the pindaric. Whereas the validity of his claims for Charles Morwent rested upon the imaginative and emotional intensity with which they were presented, the portrait of Harman Atwood and the celebration of the marriage of William and Mary were based upon empirically verifiable facts. In both these poems Oldham assumes a new role: he has metamorphosed into an observer and interpreter of data available to anyone. He is now content with 'vulgar thoughts' well expressed. Tom Brown, a contemporary writer, wittily described the 'pindaric muse' as 'a muse without her stays on': [12] Oldham's muse became more and more heavily corsetted as greater objectivity and increasing metrical regularity served him as antidotes to the enthusiastic subjectivity threatened by the mode. By 1679 the couplet had become his natural form, one more suited to his now dominant mode, the satiric.

Oldham's increased contact with the turmoil of urban life brought disillusionment that the paradigmatic values of a Harman Atwood were so little observed by men in general, a reaction perhaps fed by the strong sense of man's sinfulness fostered in him by his background. Like Lucian, Persius and Juvenal, he could not help writing satire. Satire, however, brought with it problems akin to those raised by the pindaric. Tom Brown (who claims to have known Oldham) offers a description of Oldham's satire which helps to isolate the difficulties that he faced. Brown notes that Oldham

> . . . was always in a passion; that he was inclinable to rail at everything, that both this thoughts were too furious, and his style too bold to be correct. . . . His curses were cruel, and sometimes stretched to that degree, that his verses could be termed no longer satire, but rather the hot expressions of some witty madman. [13]

Oldham does seem to have had a natural tendency to run to excess, and it scarcely needs to be said that excess of passion is at odds with the 'good sense' that he wanted to make 'the certain standard' of his poetry. He had to find some way of harnessing his natural bent without any loss of vitality. The problem that confronted him was the converse of one that Dryden had to tackle in *Absalom and Achitophel*. Whereas Dryden had to convince his readers that beneath the rational control of his poem there lurked passionate conviction, Oldham's task was to demonstrate that he was in rational command of his impetuous style. Dryden ran the risk of seeming to be so rational as to be incapable of deep feeling (and met it by appearing to let his urbane mask slip when attacking Shaftesbury's huddled procreative activities and their shapeless fruit); Oldham was in danger of seeming to be unbalanced by the force of his satiric urge. In an effort to advertise that his satiric writings rested on a firm rational and theoretical base, Oldham asserted in his preface to the *Satyrs upon the Jesuits* that he could, if he wished, 'entertain the reader with a discourse of the original, progress, and rules of satyr, and let him understand that he [had] lately read Casaubon, and several other critics upon the point': and for practical help he turned to satires by Boileau, Rochester and Dryden. In his own satires he offset the danger in several ways, by, for example, using the oblique form of a satiric monologue (as in 'Garnet's ghost'), or by adhering to a well-known model (as in his use of Horace I: viii in 'Satyr IV' of *Satyrs upon the Jesuits*), or by writing, more generally, in a particular tradition of satire (as in the two invective satires based on Archilochus and Ovid's *Ibis*). But although each of these tactics allowed Oldham to advertise rational control, none resolved the problem. Despite their variety of indirection the *Satyrs upon the Jesuits* often seem to invite a splenetic reaction in keeping with the 'rank, envenomed spleen' promised in their Prologue and quite as unbalanced as the fanatic Garnet's ghost who presses the Jesuits to be merciless in their extirpation of Protestantism:

> Spare not young infants smiling at the breast,
> Who from relenting fools their mercy wrest:
> Rip teeming wombs, tear out the hated brood
> From thence, and drown 'em in their mothers' blood.

Passages such as this seem to sound a rallying cry to a Protestant militia out to meet violence with violence. As if concerned about the rightness of such retributive justice in his paraphrase of the 137th Psalm (written at Beddington, 22 December 1676) Oldham had looked at the way in which the psalmodist had entertained a similar urge:

Bless'd, yea, thrice blessed be that barb'rous hand
(Oh grief, that I such dire revenge commend!)
Who tears out infants from their mother's womb,
And hurls them yet unborn unto their tomb:
Bless'd he who plucks them from their parents' arms,
That sanctuary from all common harms,
Who with their skulls, and bones shall pave thy streets all o'er,
And fill thy glutted channels with their scattered brains and gore.

Both Garnet's ghost and the psalmodist are depictions of unbalanced states of mind: the one is used for satiric purposes; the other is simply a portrait. Oldham recognized the usefulness of such portraiture: in the invectives against a woman and a printer, he shifts the emphasis away from satire to the satirist and sketches a picture of himself in the throes of a revengeful passion. In this way he was able to obviate any charge that the poems were direct expressions of his own revenge, 'a frailty, incident/To crazed and sickly minds', even though they are based upon retaliatory desires which he had felt. No matter how well this likeness is managed, it avoids rather than solves the problem of establishing a personal satiric voice: it is easy to see how Oldham might have felt the need to try other ways of developing a personal voice. He turned to the imitation, the adaptation of a model to modern circumstances.

In his *Essay on Translated Verse*, Roscommon was to urge:

Each poet, with a different talent writes,
One praises, one instructs, another bites.
Horace did ne'er aspire to epic bays,
Nor lofty Maro stoop to lyric lays.
Examine how your humour is inclined,
And which the ruling passion of your mind;
Then seek a poet who your way does bend,
And choose an author as you choose a friend.
United by this sympathetic bond,
You grow familiar, intimate and fond;
Your thoughts, your words, your styles, your souls agree,
No longer his interpreter, but he.[15]

Oldham explored his own propensities by imitating a variety of authors, particularly Ovid and Horace, until he found his true 'sympathetic bond' with Juvenal and his French follower Boileau. The flirtation with Ovid was brief: Oldham found that his genius tended another way and he looked to Horace, the arch-priest of that moderacy to which Oldham had turned in retreat from the enthusiasm which threatened his early work. Though Horace was an altogether happier model for Oldham, he allowed little room for that passionate intensity noted by Brown. The finest of the imitations of Horace is undoubtedly that of satire I:ix, where, in a Rochesterian vein, Oldham manages to catch something of the inflection of a contemporary sycophant; but he is more at home with the grand declamatory style of Juvenal. Horace's urbane satire presupposes that the follies attacked are temporary aberrations from a reasonable norm and that the fools are capable of being cajoled into good sense. Pope described Horace's style as 'talking on paper': like conversation, his is a social art, for he not only chats to his readers but writes from within the values of his society. By contrast Oldham felt that

> Fate has reserved us for the very lees
> Of time, where ill admits of no degrees:
> An age so bad old poets ne'er could frame,
> Nor find a metal out to give't a name.[16]

Oldham is the wolf-like moral outsider for whom sociability in the society before him is a sign of moral compromise. Fierce indignation is a much more apposite response to such a state of affairs.

As well as being heuristic, the imitation guaranteed Oldham the objectivity he so desired. The solipsist doesn't find a friend in Juvenal or Boileau, and the act of translating requires an exercise of reason beyond the enthusiast imprisoned within the bounds of his own fancy. Where the thoughts, words, styles and souls of the imitator and imitated truly agree, the imitation allows the poet to exercise his personal voice within the framework of the model, which provides both an organisational tool and a curb on excess. The voice heard in 'An allusion to Martial' is, for example, authentically Oldham: the model provided him with a means to order his thoughts. The same is true of the imitations of Juvenal, but here the greater affinity with Juvenal encouraged a greater self-exploration. In Juvenal, Oldham found a writer who, like himself, was committed to values outmoded before his birth; each was temperamentally an outsider and unable to adapt to the society in which he found himself. Because Juvenal had, in a sense, done a lot of Oldham's work for him in finding an expression for their retraction from the misvalues of their society, the later poet's energies could be devoted more to establishing the differences in their stances and to focussing the moral implications of his own. Throughout his work he had been concerned with the trinity of virtue, honour and freedom: the more disillusioned he became, the more he began to see them in stoic terms, to prize truth to the self (and God) and the freedom to enjoy that truth. Juvenal, by contrast, had been much more concerned with the extent to which he was being deprived of his material rights. The emphasis upon truth to the self in Oldham posed peculiar problems for him. Satire was his vocation: by being true to his talents as a satirist, by employing them well, he could serve his God. But the more of an outsider he became, the less he could hope to correct his age's vices and fulfil his obligations as a satirist. In the imitation of Juvenal's 13th satire, the satirist figure devotes his energies to consoling a friend who has fallen a prey to a corrupt society: that society is so hardened in its vice that his more normal reforming role is nullified, and he is reduced to complaint and trust in providence. The fears of subjectivity and enthusiasm in the earlier work are felt afresh in the later satires in the form of worries about the self-interestedness incident upon moral isolation. Outsiders, be they in Oldham or Sartre, tend to cultivate and delight in their isolation. In the imitation of Juvenal's third satire, the outburst of the poet's friend is both a satire and a portrait of the satirist as outsider. Despite the justice of his attack and his moral bearing, the old friend betrays his egotism in passage after passage, none more revealing than the following which draws a large part of its strength from the pattern of stresses on the first person pronouns:

'I live in London? What should I do there?
I cannot lie, nor flatter, nor forswear:
I can't commend a book, or piece of wit
(Though a lord were the author) dully writ:
I'm no Sir Sidrophel to read the stars,
And cast nativities for longing heirs,
When fathers shall drop off: no Gadbury
To tell the minute when the King shall die,
And you know what—come in: nor can I steer, ⎫
And tack about my conscience, whensoe'er   ⎬
To a new point, I see religion veer.   ⎭
Let others pimp to courtier's lechery,

B

I'll draw no city cuckold's curse on me:
Nor would I do it, though to be made great,
And raised to be chief Minister of State.
Therefore I think it fit to rid the town
Of one that is an useless member grown.'

In a world of egotistical nihilists, he too has come to be self-interested; his retreat is a symptom of his concern for his own rather than his society's good. The poet figure who remains behind might seem to be more balanced, but as an outsider he also is threatened by impotence in the face of a morally hostile world. Though he does not retreat, his satire, expressed through Timon, shows him more concerned to unpack his heart than to reform his fellow men. This is Oldham at his very best: the earlier strains of self-criticism and formal awareness, and his earlier attempts at the monologue portrait, here come to fruition in a study of the psychology of a representative of his own brand of satire. The imitation of Juvenal's 13th satire and the Juvenal-inspired 'Satyr concerning poetry' have similar strengths. In the light of such work it is impertinent to ask what he might have done had he lived longer. The characteristics highlighted in this introduction, together with an increased ability to pace and modulate his verse, mark him out as having a poetic personality quite independent of the other major poets of the Restoration period—Butler, Rochester and Dryden.

1. *The Poems of John Dryden*, edited by James Kinsley, 4 vols (Oxford, 1958), I, 389. [Modernised in line with other quotations.]
2. *ABC of Reading* (London, 1951), p. 151.
3. *Works of John Oldham* (London, 1686), IV, A7v.
4. *Works* (1686), II, π 3v.
5. For a full account of Oldham and the Oldhams, see my forthcoming paper in *Transactions of the Bristol and Gloucestershire Archaeological Society*.
6. John R. Jones, *The First Whigs* (London, 1961), pp. 10–11.
7. David Ogg, *England in the Reign of Charles the Second* (Oxford, 1934), p. 202.
8. Anthony a Wood, *Athenae Oxonienses*, edited by Philip Bliss, 4 vols (London, 1813–20), III, 1055–6.
9. *Works* (1686), IV, 62.
10. Bodleian MS. Rawlinson Poet 123, pp. 99–100.

11. For this and other contemporary views of Pindar, see Thomas Pope Blount, *De Re Poetica: Or Remarks upon Poetry* (London, 1694), pp. 171–4.
12. *The Works of Mr Thomas Brown*, 4 vols (London, 1760), I, 143.
13. *The Works of Mr Thomas Brown*, I, 27.
14. *Works* (1686), III, 42.
15. *An Essay on Translated Verse* (London, 1685), pp. 5–7.
16. *Works* (1686), III, 28.

Note on the Text

This selection is designed to give some indication of the range and quality of Oldham's poetry. All the pieces included are printed in full without annotation. To annotate would have been to reduce appreciably the space available for the poetry; it is hoped that readers will find that the gist of unfamiliar references is clear from their contexts.

The text is based on the third 1686 edition of Oldham's *Works*, collated with earlier editions of the *Works* and the separate parts which make up the *Works*, and Bodleian MS. Rawlinson Poet 123. The text as a whole is modernised wherever necessary, except in punctuation, which is based closely on the punctuation of the 1686 edition on the grounds that it is more sensitive to the movement of Oldham's verse than a lighter modern punctuation would be.

I should like to thank Neil Astley for his intense care in the production of this selection.

Chronological Table

1653   Born 9 August at Shipton Moyne, Gloucestershire.

1662   Father ejected from his ministry at Long Newnton, Wiltshire, close to Shipton Moyne.

1668   Begins to attend Tetbury school.

1670   Matriculates 17 June at St Edmund Hall, Oxford.

1673   Earliest extant poem, a Latin elegy on the death of his college friend John Freind, written 21 March.

1674   Leaves Oxford having taken examinations but failed to complete his degree by 'determination'. Returns to Shipton Moyne.

1675   Earliest extant English poem, a pindaric elegy on the death of his college friend Charles Morwent, written 25 August.

1676   Takes post as usher at Archbishop Whitgift School, Croydon, at some date before July. Wins patronage of Sir Nicholas Carew of Beddington who introduces his work to the Court Wits. Visited at Croydon by Rochester and several of the Wits.

1677   First appearance in print with 'Upon the marriage of the Prince of Orange with the Lady Mary', 8 November.

1678   Begins to write *Satyrs upon the Jesuits* in December.

1679   Leaves Croydon for post as tutor to Sir Edward Thurland's grandson at Reigate, Surrey, February/March. 'Garnet's ghost', the first of the *Satyrs upon the Jesuits* published in an unauthorised edition.

1681   *Satyrs upon the Jesuits . . . together with the Satyr against virtue and some other pieces by the same hand*, Oldham's first collection, appears early in year. Leaves Thurland's employment to 'set up for a wit' in London. Unsuccessful in London, takes post as tutor to the son of Sir William Hickes at Ruckholts, Low Leyton, Essex.

1681–2   Studies medicine with Richard Lower, a leading physician.

1681   *Some New Pieces . . . by the author of the Satyrs upon the Jesuits* published towards the end of the year (includes imitations of Horace).

1682   Second edition of *Some New Pieces* appears, c. May.

1682–3   Leaves Hickes's employment and returns to London.

Accepts patronage of William Pierrepont, Earl of Kingston, and moves to his seat at Holme Pierrepont, Nottinghamshire.

1683   *Poems and Translations. By the author of the Satyrs upon the Jesuits* published July (includes imitations of Juvenal and Boileau).

Dies at Holme Pierrepont, buried 7 December.

1684   First collected edition of the *Works*. 'Ode for an anniversary of music on St Cecilia's Day', set by Blow, performed for the Musical Society, 22 November.

1686   Enlarged edition of *Works*.

Bibliography

1. EDITIONS

The Works of John Oldham (1686), edited by Ken Robinson (Scholars' Facsimiles & Reprints [Delmar], available 1980).
The Poems of John Oldham, edited by Bonamy Dobrée (Centaur Press, 1960). A facsimile of the 1854 selection of Robert Bell with a new introduction: inaccurate text, notes and introduction.

2. WORKS CONTAINING POEMS BY OLDHAM NOT INCLUDED IN THE PRESENT SELECTION

Rochester's Poems on Several Occasions, edited by James Thorpe, Princeton Studies in English, 30 (Princeton University Press, 1950). Contains 'Satyr against virtue' and its 'Apology', and 'Upon the author of a play called *Sodom*'.
Poems on Affairs of State: Augustan Satirical Verse, 1660–1714, Volume II, *1678–1681*, edited by Elias F. Mengel, Jr (Yale University Press, 1965). Contains *Satyrs upon the Jesuits*.
The Gyldenstolpe Manuscript Miscellany of Poems by John Wilmot, Earl of Rochester, and other Restoration Authors, edited by Bror Danielsson and David M. Vieth, Stockholm Studies in English, 17 (Almquist and Wiksell [Stockholm], 1967). Contains 'Satyr against virtue'.
The Penguin Book of Restoration Verse, edited by Harold Love (Penguin, 1968). Contains parts of 'Satyr against virtue' and *Satyrs upon the Jesuits*, 'Upon the author of a play called *Sodom*', and the full text of 'The parting'.
Poems on Several Occasions: By the Right Honourable, the Earl of Rochester (1680) (Scolar Press, 1971). Contains 'Satyr against virtue' and its 'Apology', and 'Upon the author of a play called *Sodom*'.
Rochester, the Critical Heritage, edited by D. L. Farley-Hills (Routledge Kegan Paul, 1972). Contains Oldham's elegy.

JOHN OLDHAM
SELECTED POEMS

Complaining of absence

Ten days, if I forget not, wasted are
(A year in any lover's calendar)
Since I was forced to part, and bid adieu
To all my joy, and happiness in you;
And still by the same hinderance am detained,
Which me at first from your loved sight constrained.
Oft I resolve to meet my bliss, and then
My tether stops, and pulls me back again:
So when our raised thoughts to Heav'n aspire,
Earth stifles them, and chokes the good desire.
Curse on that man, who business first designed,
And by't enthralled a free-born lover's mind!
A curse on fate, who thus subjected me
And made me slave to anything but thee!
Lovers should be as unconfined as air,
Free as its wild inhabitants from care:
So free those happy lovers are above,
Exempt from all concerns but those of love:
But I, poor lover militant below,
The cares and troubles of dull life must know;
Must toil for that which does on others wait,
And undergo the drudgery of fate.
Yet I'll no more to her a vassal be:
Thou now shalt make and rule my destiny.
Hence troublesome fatigues! all business hence!
This very hour my freedom shall commence:
Too long that jilt has thy proud rival been,
And made me by neglectful absence sin;
But I'll no more obey its tyranny,
Nor that, nor fate itself shall hinder me,
Henceforth from seeing, and enjoying thee.

[c. September 1676]

A dithyrambic on drinking
Supposed to be spoken by Rochester at the Guinny Club.

1

Yes, you are mighty wise, I warrant, mighty wise!
  With all your godly tricks, and artifice,
Who think to chouse me of my dear and pleasant vice.
  Hence holy sham! in vain your fruitless toil:
    Go, and some inexperienced fop beguile,
    To some raw ent'ring sinner cant, and whine,
Who never knew the worth of drunkenness and wine.
  I've tried, and proved, and found it all divine:
    It is resolved: I will drink on, and die;
      I'll not one minute lose, not I,
    To hear your troublesome divinity:
Fill me a top-full glass, I'll drink it on the knee,
Confusion to the next that spoils good company!

2

  That gulp was worth a soul; like it, it went,
  And throughout new life and vigour sent:
  I feel it warm at once my head and heart,
I feel it all in all, and all in every part.
  Let the vile slaves of business toil, and strive,
  Who want the leisure, or the wit to live;
  Whilst we life's tedious journey shorter make,
  And reap those joys which they lack sense to take.
Thus live the gods (if aught above ourselves there be)
  They live so happy, unconcerned, and free:
  Like us they sit, and with a careless brow
Laugh at the petty jars of human kind below:
  Like us they spend their age in gentle ease,
Like us they drink; for what were all their Heav'n, alas!
If sober, and compelled to want that happiness.

3

Assist almighty wine, for thou alone hast power,
    And others I'll invoke no more,
  Assist, while with just praise I thee adore;

Aided by thee, I dare thy worth rehearse,
In flights above the common pitch of grovelling verse.
Thou art the world's great soul, that heavenly fire,
Which dost our dull half-kindled mass inspire.
We nothing gallant, and above ourselves produce,
Till thou dost finish man, and reinfuse.
Thou art the only source of all the world calls great,
Thou didst the poets first, and they the gods create:
To thee their rage, their heat, their flame they owe,
Thou run'st half share with art, and nature too.
They owe their glory, and renown to thee;
Thou giv'st their verse and them eternity.
Great Alexander, that bigg'st word of fame,
That fills her throat, and almost rends the same,
Whose valour found the world too strait a stage
For his wide victories and boundless rage,
Got not repute by war alone, but thee,
He knew, he ne'er could conquer by sobriety,
And drunk as well as fought for universal monarchy.

4

Pox o' that lazy claret! how it stays!
Were it again to pass the seas,
'Twould sooner be in cargo here;
'Tis now a long East-India voyage, half a year.
'Sdeath! here's a minute lost, an age, I mean,
Slipped by, and ne'er to be retrieved again.
For pity suffer not the precious juice to die,
Let us prevent our own, and its mortality:
Like it, our life with standing and sobriety is palled,
And like it too, when dead, can never be recalled.
Push on the glass, let it measure out each hour;
For every sand an health let's pour,
Swift as the rolling orbs above,
And let it too as regularly move;
Swift as heav'n's drunken red-faced traveller, the sun,
And never rest till his last race be done,
Till time itself be all run out, and we
Have drunk ourselves into eternity.

5

Six in a hand begin! We'll drink it twice apiece,
A health to all that love and honour vice.
Six more as oft to the great founder of the vine.
(A god he was, I'm sure, or should have been)
The second father of mankind I meant,
He, when the angry powers a deluge sent,
When for their crimes our sinful race was drowned,
The only bold and vent'rous man was found,
Who durst be drunk again, and with new vice the world replant.
The mighty patriarch 'twas of blessed memory,
Who 'scaped in the great wreck of all mortality,
And stocked the globe afresh with a brave drinking progeny.
In vain would spiteful nature us reclaim,
Who to small drink our isle thought fit to damn,
And set us out o' th' reach of wine,
In hope strait bounds could our vast thirst confine;
He taught us first with ships the seas to roam,
Taught us from foreign lands to fetch supply.
Rare art! that makes all the wide world our home,
Makes every realm pay tribute to our luxury.

6

Adieu poor tott'ring reason! tumble down!
This glass shall all thy proud usurping powers drown,
And wit on thy cast ruins shall erect her throne:
Adieu, thou fond disturber of our life!
That check'st our joys, with all our pleasure art at strife:
I've something brisker now to govern me,
A more exalted noble faculty,
Above thy logic, and vain boasted pedantry.
Inform me, if you can, ye reading sots, what 'tis,
That guides th'unerring deities:
They no base reason to their actions bring,
But move by some more high, more heavenly thing,
And are without deliberation wise:
Ev'n such is this, at least 'tis much the same,
For which dull schoolmen never yet could find a name.
Call ye this madness? damn that sober fool,
('Twas sure some dull philosopher, some reas'ning tool)
Who the reproachful term did first devise,
And brought a scandal on the best of vice.

Go, ask me, what's the rage young prophets feel,
    When they with holy frenzy reel:
Drunk with the spirits of infused divinity,
    They rave, and stagger, and are mad, like me.

7

    Oh, what an ebb of drink have we!
    Bring, bring a deluge, fill us up the sea,
    Let the vast ocean be our mighty cup;
We'll drink it, and all its fishes too, like loaches, up.
    Bid the Canary fleet land here: we'll pay
        The freight, and custom too defray:
    Set every man a ship, and when the store
Is emptied, let them straight dispatch, and sail for more.
        'Tis gone: and now have at the Rhine,
        With all its petty rivulets of wine:
The empire's forces with the Spanish we'll combine,
We'll make their drink too in confederacy join.
    'Ware France the next: this round Bordeaux shall swallow;
    Champagne, Langon, and Burgundy shall follow.
        Quick, let's forestall Lorraine;
        We'll starve his army, all their quarters drain,
And, without treaty put an end to the campaign.
    Go, set the universe a tilt, turn the globe up,
        Squeeze out the last, the slow unwilling drop:
    A pox of empty nature! since the world's drawn dry,
        'Tis time we quit mortality,
        'Tis time we now give out, and die,
    Lest we are plagued with dulness and sobriety.
    Beset with link-boys, we'll in triumph go,
A troop of stagg'ring ghosts, down to the shades below:
    Drunk we'll march off, and reel into the tomb,
    Nature's convenient dark retiring-room;
And there, from noise removed, and all tumultuous strife,
Sleep out the dull fatigue, and long debauch of life.

    [*Tries to go off, but tumbles down, and falls asleep.*

[5 August 1677]

c

Upon the works of Ben Jonson

Great thou! whom 'tis a crime almost to dare to praise,
Whose firm, established, and unshaken glories stand,
    And proudly their own fame command,
    Above our power to lessen or to raise,
And all, but the few heirs of thy brave genius, and thy bays;
Hail mighty founder of our stage! for so I dare
    Entitle thee, nor any modern censures fear,
    Nor care what thy unjust detractors say.
They'll say, perhaps, that others did materials bring,
    That others did the first foundations lay,
    And glorious 'twas (we grant) but to begin,
    But thou alone couldst finish the design,
All the fair model, and the workmanship was thine:
    Some bold advent'rers might have been before,
      Who durst the unknown world explore;
    By them it was surveyed at distant view,
    And here and there a Cape, and Line they drew,
    Which only served as hints, and marks to thee,
Who wast reserved to make the full discovery.
    Art's compass to thy painful search we owe,
    Whereby thou went'st so far, and we may after go:
By that we may wit's vast and trackless ocean try,
      Content no longer, as before,
      Dully to coast along the shore,
    But steer a course more unconfined, and free,
Beyond the narrow bounds that pent antiquity.

2

Never till thee the theatre possessed
A prince with equal power and greatness blessed;
    No government, or laws it had
    To strengthen and establish it,
    Till thy great hand the sceptre swayed,
But groaned under a wretched anarchy of wit:
    Unformed, and void was then its poesy,
    Only some pre-existing matter we
      Perhaps could see,
    That might foretell what was to be;

A rude and undigested lump it lay,
Like the old chaos, e'er the birth of light and day,
Till thy brave genius like a new creator came,
And undertook the mighty frame.
No shuffled atoms did the well-built work compose,
It from no lucky hit of blund'ring chance arose
(As some of this great fabric idly dream)
But wise, all seeing judgment did contrive,
And knowing art its graces give:
No sooner did thy soul with active force and fire
The dull and heavy mass inspire,
But straight throughout it let us see
Proportion, order, harmony,
And every part did to the whole agree,
And straight appeared a beauteous, new-made world of poetry.

3

Let dull and ignorant pretenders art condemn;
(Those only foes to art, and art to them)
The mere fanatics, and enthusiasts in poetry,
(For schismatics in that, as in religion be)
Who make't all revelation, trance, and dream;
Let them despise her laws, and think
That rules and forms the spirit stint:
Thine was no mad, unruly frenzy of the brain,
Which justly might deserve the chain,
'Twas brisk, and mettled, but a managed rage;
Sprightly as vig'rous youth, and cool as temp'rate age:
Free, like thy will, it did all force disdain,
But suffered reason's loose, and easy rein,
By that it suffered to be led,
Which did not curb poetic liberty, but guide:
Fancy, that wild and haggard faculty,
Untamed in most, and let at random fly,
Was wisely governed, and reclaimed by thee;
Restraint and discipline was made endure,
And by thy calm and milder judgment brought to lure;
Yet when 'twas at some nobler quarry sent,
With bold, and tow'ring wings it upwards went,
Not lessened at the greatest height,
Not turned by the most giddy flights of dazzling wit.

4

Nature, and art, together met, and joined,
Made up the character of thy great mind.
That, like a bright and glorious sphere,
Appeared with numerous stars embellished o'er,
And much of light to thee, and much of influence bore;
This, was the strong intelligence, whose power
Turned it about, and did the unerring motions steer:
Concurring both, like vital seed, and heat,
The noble births they jointly did beget,
And hard 'twas to be thought,
Which most of force to the great generation brought.
So mingling elements compose our bodies' frame,
Fire, water, earth, and air,
Alike their just proportions share,
Each undistinguished still remains the same,
Yet can't we say that either's here, or there,
But all, we know not how, are scattered everywhere.

5

Sober and grave was still the garb thy muse put on,
No tawdry careless slattern dress,
Nor starched, and formal with affectedness,
Nor the cast mode, and fashion of the court and town;
But neat, agreeable, and jaunty 'twas,
Well fitted, it sat close in every place,
And all became, with an uncommon air and grace:
Rich, costly and substantial was the stuff,
Not barely smooth, nor yet too coarsely rough:
No refuse, ill-patched shreds o' th' schools,
The motley wear of read and learned fools,
No French commodity which now so much does take,
And our own better manufacture spoil;
Nor was it aught of foreign soil,
But staple all, and all of English growth and make:
What flowers soe'er of art it had, were found
No tinsel slight embroideries,
But all appeared either the native ground,
Or twisted, wrought, and interwoven with the piece.

6

Plain humour, shown with her whole various face,
  Not masked with any antic dress,
Nor screwed in forced ridiculous grimace
  (The gaping rabble's dull delight,
And more the actor's than the poet's wit)
  Such did she enter on thy stage,
And such was represented to the wond'ring age:
Well wast thou skilled and read in human kind,
In every wild fantastic passion of his mind,
Didst into all his hidden inclinations dive,
  What each from nature does receive,
Or age, or sex, or quality, or country give;
  What custom too, that mighty sorceress,
  Whose powerful witchcraft does transform
Enchanted man to several monstrous images,
  Makes this an odd, and freakish monkey turn,
  And that a grave and solemn ass appear,
And all a thousand beastly shapes of folly wear:
  Whate'er caprice or whimsey leads awry
  Perverted, and seduced mortality,
    Or does incline, and bias it
From what's discreet, and wise, and right, and good and fit;
  All in thy faithful glass were so expressed,
  As if they were reflections of thy breast,
  As if they had been stamped on thy own mind,
And thou the universal vast idea of mankind.

7

Never didst thou with the same dish repeated cloy,
  Though every dish, well-cooked by thee,
  Contained a plentiful variety:
  To all that could sound relishing palates be,
Each regale with new delicacies did invite,
  Courted the taste, and raised the appetite:
  Whate'er fresh dainty fops in season were,
  To garnish and set out thy bill of fare
  (Those never found to fail throughout the year,
  For seldom that ill-natured planet rules,
  That plagues a poet with a dearth of fools)
  What thy strict observation e'er surveyed,
From the fine, luscious spark of high and courtly breed,

Down to the dull, insipid cit,
Made thy pleased audience entertainment fit,
Served up with all the grateful poignancies of wit.

8

Most plays are writ like almanacks of late,
And serve one only year, one only state;
Another makes them useless, stale, and out of date;
But thine were wisely calculated fit
For each meridian, every clime of wit,
For all succeeding time, and after-age,
And all mankind might thy vast audience sit,
And the whole world be justly made thy stage:
Still they shall taking be, and ever new,
Still keep in vogue in spite of all the damning crew;
Till the last scene of this great theatre,
Closed, and shut down,
The numerous actors all retire,
And the grand play of human life be done.

9

Beshrew those envious tongues who seek to blast thy bays,
Who spots in thy bright fame would find, or raise,
And say it only shines with borrowed rays;
Rich in thyself, to whose unbounded store
Exhausted nature could vouchsafe no more,
Thou couldst alone the empire of the stage maintain,
Couldst all its grandeur, and its port sustain,
Nor needest others subsidies to pay,
Needest no tax on foreign, or thy native country lay,
To bear the charges of thy purchased fame,
But thy own stock could raise the same,
Thy sole revenue all the vast expense defray:
Yet, like some mighty conqueror in poetry,
Designed by fate of choice to be
Founder of its new universal monarchy,
Boldly thou didst the learned world invade,
Whilst all around thy powerful genius swayed,
Soon vanquished Rome, and Greece were made submit,
Both were thy humble tributaries made,
And thou return'dst in triumph with their captive wit.

10

Unjust, and more ill-natured those,
Thy weak but spiteful and malicious foes
Who on thy happiest talent fix a lie,
And call that slowness, which was care, and industry.
Let me (with pride so to be guilty thought)
Share all thy wished reproach, and share thy shame,
If diligence be deemed a fault,
If to be faultless must deserve their blame:
Judge of thyself alone (for none there were,
Could be so just, or could be so severe)
Thou thy own works didst strictly try
By known and uncontested rules of poetry,
And gav'st thy sentence still impartially:
With rigour thou arraign'dst each guilty line,
And didst of each offending word define,
And spar'dst no criminal sense, because 'twas thine:
Unbribed by favour, love or self-conceit
(For never, or too seldom we,
Objects too near us, our own blemishes can see)
Thou didst no small'st delinquencies acquit,
But saw'st them to correction all submit,
Saw'st execution done on all convicted crimes of wit.

11

Some curious painter, taught by art to dare
(For they with poets in that title share)
When he would undertake a glorious frame
Of lasting worth, and fadeless as his fame,
Long he contrives, and weighs the bold design,
Long holds his doubting hand e'er he begin,
And justly then proportions every stroke, and line,
And oft he brings it to review,
And oft he does deface, and dashes oft anew,
And mixes oil to make the flitting colours dure,
To keep 'em from the tarnish of injurious time secure;
Finished at length in all that care and skill can do,
The matchless piece is set to public view,
And all surprised about it wond'ring stand,
And though no name be found below,
Yet straight discern th'inimitable hand,
And straight they cry 'tis Titian, or 'tis Angelo:

So thy brave soul, that scorned all cheap, and easy ways,
    And trod no common road to praise,
Would not with rash, and speedy negligence proceed
    (For whoe'er saw perfection grow in haste?
    Or that soon done, which must for ever last?)
    But gently did advance with wary heed,
And shewed that mastery is most in justness read :
Nought ever issued from thy teeming breast,
But what had gone full time, could write exactly best,
And stand the sharpest censure, and defy the rigid'st test.

12

    'Twas thus th'Almighty Poet (if we dare
    Our weak, and meaner acts with His compare)
When He the world's fair poem did of old design,
    That work, which now must boast no longer date than thine,
    Though 'twas in Him alike to will, and do,
    Though the same Word that spoke, could make it too,
Yet would He not such quick, and hasty methods use,
Nor did an instant (which it might) the great effect produce;
    But when th'All-wise himself in council sat,
    Vouchsafed to think and be deliberate,
When Heav'n considered, and th'Eternal Wit and Sense,
    Seemed to take time, and care, and pains,
    It shewed that some uncommon birth,
That something worthy of a God was coming forth;
    Nought incorrect there was, nought faulty there,
No point amiss did in the large voluminous piece appear;
    And when the glorious Author all surveyed,
    Surveyed whate'er His mighty labours made,
    Well pleased He was to find
All answered the great model and idea of His mind :
    Pleased at himself He in high wonder stood,
    And much His power, and much His wisdom did applaud,
To see how all was perfect, all transcendent good.

13

Let meaner spirits stoop to low precarious fame,
    Content on gross and coarse applause to live,
    And what the dull and senseless rabble give;
    Thou didst it still with noble scorn contemn,

Nor wouldst that wretched alms receive,
The poor subsistence of some bankrupt, sordid name:
Thine was no empty vapour, raised beneath,
    And formed of common breath,
The false, and foolish fire, that's whisked about
By popular air, and glares a while, and then goes out;
But 'twas a solid, whole, and perfect globe of light,
That shone all over, was all over bright,
And dared all sullying clouds, and feared no dark'ning night;
Like the gay monarch of the stars and sky,
    Who wheresoe'er he does display
His sovereign lustre, and majestic ray,
Straight all the less, and petty glories nigh
    Vanish, and shrink away,
O'erwhelmed, and swallowed by the greater blaze of day;
With such a strong, an awful and victorious beam
Appeared, and ever shall appear, thy fame,
Viewed, and adored, by all th'undoubted race of wit,
    Who only can endure to look on it,
    The rest o'ercome with too much light,
With too much brightness dazzled, or extinguished quite.
Restless, and uncontrolled it now shall pass
As wide a course about the world as he,
And when his long-repeated travels cease,
    Begin a new, and vaster race,
And still tread round the endless circle of eternity.

[early 1678]

A satyr upon a woman who by her falsehood and scorn was the death of my friend

No! she shall ne'er escape, if Gods there be,
Unless they perjured grow, and false as she;
Though no strange judgment yet the murderess seize
To punish her, and quit the partial skies;
Though no revenging lightning yet has flashed
From thence, that might her criminal beauties blast;
Though they in their old lustre still prevail,
By no disease, nor guilt itself made pale,
Guilt, which, should blackest Moors themselves but own,
Would make through all their night new blushes dawn:
Though that kind soul, who now augments the blest,
Thither too soon by her unkindness chased,
(Where may it be her small'st and lightest doom—
For that's not half my curse—never to come)
Though he, when prompted by the high'st despair,
Ne'er mentioned her without an hymn or prayer,
And could by all her scorn be forced no more
Than martyrs to revile what they adore;
Who had he cursed her with his dying breath
Had done but just, and Heaven had forgave,
Though ill-made Law no sentence has ordained
For her, no statute has her guilt arraigned
(For hangmen, women's scorn, and doctors' skill,
All by a licensed way of murder kill).
Though she from justice of all these go free,
And boasts perhaps in her success, and cry:
'Twas but a little harmless perjury;
Yet think she not she still secure shall prove,
Or that none dare avenge an injured love:
I rise in judgment, am to be to her
Both witness, judge, and executioner.
Armed with dire satyr, and resentful spite,
I come to haunt her with the ghosts of wit.
My ink unbid starts out, and flies on her,
Like blood upon some touching murderer;
And should that fail, rather than want, I would,
Like hags, to curse her, write in my own blood.
   Ye spiteful powers (if any there can be
That boast a worse and keener spite than I)

Assist with malice and your mighty aid
My sworn revenge, and help me rhyme her dead:
Grant I may fix such brands of infamy,
So plain, so deeply graved on her, that she,
Her skill, patches, nor paint, all joined can hide,
And which shall lasting as her soul abide.
Grant my strong hate may such strong poison cast,
That every breath may taint, and rot, and blast,
Till one large gangrene quite o'erspread her fame
With foul contagion; till her odious name,
Spit at, and cursed by every mouth like mine,
Be terror to herself and all her line.
  Vilest of that viler sex, who damned us all!
Ordained to cause, and plague us for our fall!
Woman! nay worse! for she can nought be said
But mummy by some devil inhabited:
Not made in Heaven's mint, but basely coined,
She wears an human image stamped on fiend;
And whoso marriage would with her contract,
Is witch by law, and that a mere compact.
Her soul (if any soul in her there be)
By Hell was breathed into her in a lie,
And its whole stock of falsehood there was lent,
As if hereafter to be true it meant.
Bawd Nature taught her jilting when she made,
And by her make, designed her for the trade:
Hence 'twas she daubed her with a painted face,
That she at once might better cheat and please.
All those gay charming looks that court the eye
Are but an ambush to hide treachery;
Mischief adorned with pomp, and smooth disguise,
A painted skin stuffed full of guise and lies;
Within a gaudy case, a nasty soul,
Like turd of quality in a gilt close-stool:
Such on a cloud those flattering colours are,
Which only serve to dress a tempest fair.
So men upon this Earth's fair surface dwell,
Within are fiends, and at the centre Hell:
Court-promises, the leagues which statesmen make
With more convenience, and more ease to break,
The faith a Jesuit in allegiance swears,
Or a town-jilt to keeping coxcombs bears,
Are firm, and certain all, compared with hers:
Early in falsehood, at her font, she lied,
And should ev'n then for perjury been tried:

Her conscience stretched, and open as the stews,
But laughs at oaths, and plays with solemn vows;
And at her mouth swallows down perjured breath,
More glib than bits of lechery beneath:
Less serious known when she doth most protest,
Than thoughts of arrantest buffoons in jest:
More cheap than the vile mercenariest Squire
That plies for half-crown fees at Westminster,
And trades in staple oaths, and swears to hire:
Less guilt than hers, less breach of oath, and word,
Has stood aloft and looked through penance board;
And he that trusts her in a death-bed prayer
Has faith to merit, and save anything, but her.
     But since her guilt description does outgo,
I'll try if it outstrip my curses too;
Curses, which may they equal my just hate,
My wish, and her desert, be each so great,
Each heard like prayers, and Heaven make 'em fate.
     First, for her beauties, which the mischief brought:
May she affected, they be borrowed thought,
By her own hand, not that of Nature wrought:
Her credit, honour, portion, health, and those
Prove light, and frail, as her broke faith, and vows.
Some base, unnamed disease her carcase foul,
And make her body ugly as her soul:
Cankers, and ulcers eat her, till she be
Shunned like infection, loathed like infamy.
Strength quite expired, may she alone retain
The snuff of life, may that unquenched remain,
As in the damned, to keep her fresh for pain:
Hot lust light on her, and the plague of pride
On that: this ever scorned, as that denied.
Ache, anguish, horror, grief, dishonour, shame,
Pursue at once her body, soul and fame.
If e'er the devil-love must enter her
(For nothing sure but fiends can enter there)
May she a just and true tormenter find,
And that, like an ill conscience, rack her mind.
Be some diseased and ugly wretch her fate,
She doomed to love of one whom all else hate.
May he hate her, and may her destiny
Be to despair, and yet love on and die;
Or, to invent some wittier punishment,
May he, to plague her, out of spite consent;

May the old fumbler, though disabled quite,
Have strength to give her claps, but no delight:
May he of her unjustly jealous be
For one that's worse, and uglier far than he:
May's impotence balk and torment her lust,
Yet scarcely her to dreams or wishes trust:
Forced to be chaste, may she suspected be,
Share none o' th' pleasure, all the infamy.
   In fine, that I all curses may complete
(For I've but cursed in jest, raillied yet)
Whate'er the sex deserves, or feels, or fears,
May all those plagues be hers, and only hers;
Whate'er great favourites turned out of doors,
Shamed cullies, bilked and disappointed whores,
Or losing gamesters vent, what curses e'er
Are spoke by sinners raving in despair:
All those fall on her, as they're all her due,
Till spite can't think, nor Heav'n inflict anew:
May then (for once I will be kind, and pray)
No madness take her use of sense away;
But may she in full strength of reason be,
To feel and understand her misery;
Plagued so, till she think damning a release,
And humbly pray to go to Hell for ease.
Yet may not all these sufferings here atone
Her sin, and may she still go sinning on,
Tick up in perjury, and run o' th' score
Till on her soul she can get trust no more:
   Then may she stupid and repentless die,
And Heav'n itself forgive no more than I,
But so be damned of mere necessity.

[Whitsuntide 1678]

A letter out of the country to a friend in town
giving an account of the author's inclinations to poetry

As to that poet (if so great a one as he,
May suffer in comparison with me)
When heretofore in Scythian exile pent,
To which he from ungrateful Rome was sent:
If a kind paper from his country came,
And wore subscribed some known and faithful name,
That, like a powerful cordial, did infuse
New life into his speechless gasping muse,
And straight his genius, which before did seem
Bound up in ice, and frozen as the clime,
By its warm force and friendly influence thawed,
Dissolved apace, and in soft numbers flowed:
Such welcome here, dear sir, your letter had
With me, shut up in close constraint as bad:
Not eager lovers, held in long suspense,
With warmer joy, and a more tender sense,
Meet those kind lines which all their wishes bless,
And sign, and seal delivered happiness:
My grateful thoughts so throng to get abroad,
They overrun each other in the crowd:
To you with hasty flight they take their way,
And hardly for the dress of words will stay.
    Yet pardon, if this only fault I find,
That while you praise too much, you are less kind:
Consider, sir, 'tis ill and dang'rous thus
To over-lay a young and tender muse:
Praise, the fine diet which we're apt to love,
If given to excess, does hurtful prove:
Where it does weak, distempered stomachs meet,
That surfeits, which should nourishment create.
Your rich perfumes such fragrancy dispense,
Their sweetness overcomes and palls my sense;
On my weak head you heap so many bays,
I sink beneath 'em, quite oppressed with praise,
And a resembling fate with him receive,
Who in too kind a triumph found his grave,
Smothered with garlands, which applauders gave.
    To you these praises justlier all belong,
By alienating which yourself you wrong:

Whom better can such commendations fit
Than you, who so well teach and practise wit?
Verse, the great boast of drudging fools, from some,
Nay most of scribblers, with much straining come:
They void 'em dribbling, and in pain they write,
As if they had a stranguary of wit:
Your pen, uncalled they readily obey,
And scorn your ink should flow so fast as they:
Each strain of yours so easy does appear,
Each such a graceful negligence does wear,
As shews you have none, and yet want no care:
None of your serious pains or time they cost,
But what thrown by, you can afford for lost.
If such the fruits of your loose leisure be,
Your careless minutes yield such poetry,
We guess what proofs your genius would impart,
Did it employ you, as it does divert:
But happy you, more prudent, and more wise,
With better aims have fixed your noble choice.
While silly I all thriving arts refuse,
And all my hopes, and all my vigour lose
In service on that worst of jilts, a muse,
For gainful business court ignoble ease,
And in gay trifles waste my ill-spent days.
    Little I thought, my dearest friend, that you
Would thus contribute to my ruin too:
O'errun with filthy poetry and rhyme,
The present reigning evil of the time,
I lacked, and (well I did myself assure)
From your kind hand I should receive a cure:
When, lo! instead of healing remedies,
You cherish, and encourage the disease:
Inhuman, you help the distemper on,
Which was before but too inveterate grown:
As a kind looker on, who int'rest shares,
Though not in's stake, yet in his hopes and fears,
Would to his friend a pushing gamester do,
Recall his elbow when he hastes to throw;
Such a wise course you should have took with me,
A rash and vent'ring fool in poetry.
Poets are cullies, whom rook fame draws in,
And wheedles with deluding hopes to win:
But, when they hit, and most successful are,
They scarce come off with a bare saving share.

Oft, I remember, did wise friends dissuade,
And bid me quit the trifling barren trade:
Oft have I tried (Heaven knows) to mortify
This vile and wicked lust of poetry;
But still unconquered it remains within,
Fixed as an habit, or some darling sin.
In vain, I better studies there would sow,
Often I've tried, but none will thrive or grow:
All my best thoughts, when I'd most serious be,
Are never from its foul infection free:
Nay (God forgive me) when I say my prayers,
I scarce can help polluting them with verse:
That fabulous wretch of old reversed I seem,
Who turn whate'er I touch to dross and rhyme.
  Oft, to divert the wild caprice, I try
If sovereign wisdom and philosophy
Rightly applied, will give a remedy:
Straight the great Stagyrite I take in hand,
Seek nature, and myself to understand:
Much I reflect on his vast worth and fame,
And much my low and grovelling aims condemn,
And quarrel, that my ill-packed fate should be
This vain, this worthless thing called poetry:
But when I find this unregarded toy
Could his important thoughts and pains employ,
By reading there, I am but more undone,
And meet that danger which I went to shun.
Oft when ill humour, chagrin, discontent,
Give leisure my wild follies to resent,
I thus against myself my passion vent:
'Enough, mad rhyming sot, enough for shame,
Give o'er, and all thy quills to tooth-picks damn;
Didst ever thou the altar rob, or worse,
Kill the priest there, and maids receiving force?
What else could merit this so heavy curse?
The greatest curse I can, I wish on him,
(If there be any greater than to rhyme)
Who first did of the lewd invention think,
First made two lines with sounds resembling clink,
And, swerving from the easy paths of prose,
Fetters and chains did on free sense impose:
Cursed too be all the fools, who since have went
Misled in steps of that ill precedent:
Want be entailed their lot:'——and on I go,
Wreaking my spite on all the jingling crew:

Scarce the beloved Cowley 'scapes, though I
Might sooner my own curses fear, than he:
And thus resolved against the scribbling vein,
I deeply swear never to write again.
  But when bad company and wine conspire
To kindle and renew the foolish fire,
Straightways relapsed, I feel the raving fit
Return, and straight I all my oaths forget:
The spirit, which I thought cast out before,
Enters again with stronger force and power,
Worse than at first, and tyrannizes more.
No sober good advice will then prevail,
Nor from the raging frenzy me recall:
Cool reason's dictates me no more can move
Than men in drink, in Bedlam, or in love:
Deaf to all means which might most proper seem
Towards my cure, I run stark mad in rhyme:
A sad poor haunted wretch, whom nothing less
Than prayers of the Church can dispossess.
  Sometimes, after a tedious day half spent,
When fancy long has hunted on cold scent,
Tired in the dull and fruitless chase of thought,
Despairing I grow weary, and give out:
As a dry lecher pumped of all my store,
I loathe the thing, 'cause I can do't no more:
But, when I once begin to find again
Recruits of matter in my pregnant brain,
Again, more eager I the hunt pursue,
And with fresh vigour the loved sport renew:
Tickled with some strange pleasure, which I find,
And think a secrecy to all mankind,
I please myself with the vain, false delight,
And count none happy, but the fops that write.
  'Tis endless, sir, to tell the many ways
Wherein my poor deluded self I please:
How, when the fancy lab'ring for a birth,
With unfelt throes brings its rude issue forth:
How after, when imperfect shapeless thought
Is by the judgment into fashion wrought;
When at first search I traverse o'er my mind,
Nought but a dark and empty void I find:
Some little hints at length, like sparks, break thence,
And glimm'ring thoughts just dawning into sense:
Confused a while the mixed ideas lie,
With nought of mark to be discovered by,

D

Like colours undistinguished in the night,
Till the dusk images, moved to the light,
Teach the discerning faculty to choose,
Which it had best adopt, and which refuse.
Here rougher strokes, touched with a careless dash,
Resemble the first sitting of a face:
There finished draughts in form more full appear,
And to their justness ask no further care.
Meanwhile with inward joy I proud am grown,
To see the work successfully go on:
And prize myself in a creating power
That could make something, what was nought before.
   Sometimes a stiff, unwieldly thought I meet,
Which to my laws will scarce be made submit:
But when, after expense of pains and time,
'Tis managed well, and taught to yoke in rhyme,
I triumph more than joyful warriors would,
Had they some stout, and hardy foe subdued,
And idly think, less goes to their command,
That makes armed troops in well-placed order stand,
Than to the conduct of my words, when they
March in due ranks, are set in just array.
   Sometimes on wings of thought I seem on high,
As men in sleep, though motionless they lie,
Fledged by a dream, believe they mount and fly:
So witches some enchanted wand bestride,
And think they through the airy regions ride,
Where fancy is both traveller, way, and guide:
Then straight I grow a strange exalted thing,
And equal in conceit at least a king:
As the poor drunkard, when wine stums his brains,
Anointed with that liquor, thinks he reigns.
Bewitched by these delusions 'tis I write,
(The tricks some pleasant devil plays in spite)
And when I'm in the freakish trance, which I,
Fond silly wretch, mistake for ecstasy,
I find all former resolutions vain,
And thus recant them, and make new again:
   'What was't I rashly vowed? shall ever I
Quit my beloved mistress, poetry?
Thou sweet beguiler of my lonely hours,
Which thus glide unperceived with silent course;
Thou gentle spell, which undisturbed dost keep
My breast, and charm intruding care asleep:

They say, thou'rt poor and unendowed; what though?
For thee, I this vain, worthless world forego:
Let wealth and honour be for fortune's slaves,
The alms of fools, and prize of crafty knaves:
To me thou art whate'er the ambitious crave,
And all that greedy misers want, or have:
In youth or age, in travel or at home,
Here, or in town, at London, or at Rome,
Rich, or a beggar, free, or in the Fleet,
Whate'er my fate is, 'tis my fate to write.'
    Thus I have made my shrifted muse confess,
Her secret feebles and her weaknesses:
All her hid faults she sets exposed to view,
And hopes a gentle confessor in you:
She hopes an easy pardon for her sin,
Since 'tis but what she is not wilful in,
Nor yet has scandalous nor open been.
Try if your ghostly counsel can reclaim
The heedless wanton from her guilt and shame:
At least be not ungenerous to reproach
That wretched frailty which you've helped debauch.
    'Tis now high time to end, for fear I grow
More tedious than old doters, when they woo,
Than travelled fops, when far-fetched lies they prate,
Or flattering poets, when they dedicate.
No dull forgiveness I presume to crave,
Nor vainly for my tiresome length ask leave:
Lest I, as often formal coxcombs use,
Prolong that very fault I would excuse:
May this the same kind welcome find with you,
As yours did here, and ever shall; adieu.

[July 1678]

The careless good-fellow

1

A pox of this fooling and plotting of late,
What a pother and stir has it kept in the state!
Let the rabble run mad with suspicions and fears,
Let them scuffle, and jar, till they go by the ears:
  Their grievances never shall trouble my pate,
  So I can enjoy my dear bottle at quiet.

2

What coxcombs were those, who would barter their ease
And their necks for a toy, a thin wafer and mass!
At old Tyburn they never had needed to swing,
Had they been but true subjects to drink, and their king:
  A friend and a bottle is all my design;
  He has no room for treason, that's top-full of wine.

3

I mind not the members and makers of laws,
Let them sit or prorogue, as his majesty please:
Let them damn us to woollen, I'll never repine
At my lodging when dead, so alive I have wine:
  Yet oft in my drink I can hardly forbear
  To curse them for making my claret so dear.

4

I mind not grave asses who idly debate
About right and succession, the trifles of state;
We've a good king already; and he deserves laughter
That will trouble his head with who shall come after:
  Come, here's to his health, and I wish he may be
  As free from all care and all trouble as we.

5

What care I how leagues with the Hollander go?
Or intrigues betwixt Sidney and Monsieur D'Avaux?
What concerns it my drinking if Cassel be sold,
If the conqueror take it by storming, or gold?
   Good Bordeaux alone is the place that I mind,
   And when the fleet's coming, I pray for a wind.

6

The bully of France, that aspires to renown
By dull cutting of throats, and vent'ring his own,
Let him fight and be damned, and make matches and treat,
To afford the newsmongers, and coffee-house chat:
   He's but a brave wretch, while I am more free,
   More safe, and a thousand times happier than he.

7

Come He, or the Pope, or the Devil to boot,
Or come faggot, and stake; I care not a groat;
Never think that in Smithfield I porters will heat:
No, I swear, Mr Fox, pray excuse me for that.
   I'll drink in defiance of gibbet and halter,
   This is the profession that never will alter.

[9 March 1680]

An imitation of Horace
Book I: satyr IX

As I was walking in the Mall of late,
Alone, and musing on I know not what,
Comes a familiar fop, whom hardly I
Knew by his name, and rudely seizes me:
'Dear sir, I'm mighty glad to meet with you;
And pray, how have you done this age, or two?'
'Well, I thank God,' said I, 'as times are now:
I wish the same to you.' And so passed on,
Hoping with this, the coxcomb would be gone.
But when I saw I could not thus get free,
I asked, what business else he had with me.
'Sir,' answered he, 'if learning, parts, or sense
Merit your friendship, I have just pretence.'
'I honour you,' said I, 'upon that score,
And shall be glad to serve you to my power.'
Meantime, wild to get loose, I try all ways
To shake him off: sometimes I walk apace,
Sometimes stand still; I frown, I chafe, I fret,
Shrug, turn my back, as in the Bagnio, sweat;
And show all kinds of signs to make him guess
At my impatience and uneasiness.
'Happy the folk in Newgate!' whispered I,
'Who, though in chains, are from this torment free:
Would I were like rough Manly in the play,
To send impertinents with kicks away!'
He all the while baits me with tedious chat,
Speaks much about the drought, and how the rate
Of hay is raised, and what it now goes at:
Tells me of a new comet at the Hague,
Portending God knows what, a dearth, or plague:
Names every wench that passes through the park,
How much she is allowed, and who the spark
That keeps her: points who lately got a clap,
And who at the groom-porters had ill hap
Three nights ago, in play with such a lord.
When he observed I minded not a word,
And did no answer to his trash afford,
'Sir, I perceive you stand on thorns,' said he,
'And fain would part; but, faith, it must not be:

Come, let us take a bottle.' I cried, 'No,
Sir, I am in a course, and dare not now.'
'Then tell me whither you desire to go:
I'll wait upon you.' 'Oh! sir, 'tis too far:
I visit cross the water: therefore spare
Your needless trouble.' 'Trouble! sir, 'tis none:
'Tis more by half to leave you here alone.
I have no present business to attend,
At least, which I'll not quit for such a friend.
Tell me not of the distance; for, I vow,
I'll cut the Line, double the Cape for you:
Good faith, I will not leave you; make no words.
Go you to Lambeth? Is it to my Lord's?
His steward I most intimately know,
Have often drunk with his comptroller too.'
By this I found my wheedle would not pass,
But rather served my suff'rings to increase;
And seeing 'twas in vain to vex, or fret,
I patiently submitted to my fate.
   Straight he begins again: 'Sir, if you knew
My worth but half so thoroughly as I do,
I'm sure, you would not value any friend
You have, like me: but that I won't commend
Myself, and my own talents, I might tell
How many ways to wonder I excel.
None has a greater gift in poetry,
Or writes more verses with more ease than I:
I'm grown the envy of the men of wit,
I killed even Rochester with grief and spite:
Next for the dancing part, I all surpass,
St André never moved with such a grace;
And 'tis well known, whene'er I sing, or set,
Humphreys, nor Blow, could ever match me yet.'
   Here I got room to interrupt: 'Have you
A mother, sir, or kindred living now?'
'Not one: they are all dead.' 'Troth, so I guessed:
The happier they,' said I, 'who are at rest:
Poor I am only left unmurdered yet:
Haste, I beseech you, and despatch me quite,
For I am well convinced, my time is come:
When I was young, a gipsy told my doom:
This lad (said she, and looked upon my hand)
Shall not by sword, or poison come to's end,
Nor by the fever, dropsy, gout, or stone,
But he shall die by an eternal tongue:

Therefore, when he's grown up, if he be wise,
Let him avoid great talkers, I advise.'
  By this time we were got to Westminster,
Where he by chance a trial had to hear,
And, if he were not there, his cause must fall:
'Sir, if you love me, step into the Hall
For one half-hour.' 'The devil take me now,'
Said I, 'if I know anything of law:
Besides, I told you whither I'm to go.'
Hereat he made a stand, pulled down his hat
Over his eyes, and mused in deep debate:
'I'm in a strait,' said he, 'what I shall do:
Whether forsake my business, sir, or you.'
'Me by all means,' say I. 'No,' says my sot,
'I fear you'll take it ill, if I should do't:
I'm sure you will.' 'Not I, by all that's good,
But I've more breeding, than to be so rude.
Pray, don't neglect your own concerns for me:
Your cause, good sir!' 'My cause be damned,' says he,
'I value't less than your dear company.'
With this he came up to me, and would lead
The way; I, sneaking after, hung my head.
  Next he begins to plague me with the plot,
Asks, whether I were known to Oates or not?
'Not I, thank Heaven! I no priest have been,
Have never Douay, nor St Omer seen.'
'What think you, sir: will they the Joiner try?
Will he die, think you?' 'Yes, most certainly.'
'I mean, be hanged.' 'Would thou wert so,' wished I!
Religion came in next; though he'd no more
Than the French King, his punk, or confessor:
'Oh! the sad times, if once the King should die!
Sir, are you not afraid of popery?'
'No more than my superiors: why should I?
I've no estate in abbey-lands to lose.'
'But fire and faggot, sir, how like you those?'
'Come Inquisition, anything,' thought I,
'So heaven would bless me to get rid of thee!
But 'tis some comfort, that my Hell is here:
I need no punishment hereafter fear.'
  Scarce had I thought, but he falls on anew:
'How stands it, sir, betwixt his Grace and you?'
'Sir, he's a man of sense above the crowd,
And shuns the converse of a multitude.'

'Ay, sir,' says he, 'you're happy who are near
His Grace, and have the favour of his ear;
But let me tell you, if you'll recommend
This person here, your point will soon be gained.
Gad, sir, I'll die, if my own single wit
Don't fob his minions, and displace 'em quite;
And make yourself his only favourite.'
'No, you are out abundantly,' said I,
'We live not, as you think: no family
Throughout the whole three kingdoms is more free
From those ill customs, which are used to swarm
In great men's houses; none e'er does me harm,
Because more learned, or more rich than I;
But each man keeps his place, and his degree.'
' 'Tis mighty strange,' says he, 'what you relate.'
'But nothing truer, take my word for that.'
'You make me long to be admitted too
Amongst his creatures: Sir, I beg, that you
Will stand my friend: your interest is such,
You may prevail. I'm sure you can do much:
He's one that may be won upon, I've heard,
Though at the first approach access be hard.
I'll spare no trouble of my own, or friends,
No cost in fees, and bribes to gain my ends:
I'll seek all opportunities to meet
With him, accost him in the very street,
Hang on his coach, and wait upon him home,
Fawn, scrape and cringe to him, nay, to his groom.
Faith, sir, this must be done, if we'll be great:
Preferment comes not at a cheaper rate.'
    While at this savage rate he worried me,
By chance a doctor, my dear friend, came by,
That knew the fellow's humour passing well:
Glad of the sight, I join him; we stand still:
'Whence came you, sir? and whither go you now?'
And such like questions passed betwixt us two.
Straight I begin to pull him by the sleeve,
Nod, wink upon him, touch my nose, and give
A thousand hints, to let him know that I
Needed his help for my delivery:
He, naughty wag, with an arch fleering smile,
Seems ignorant of what I mean the while.
I grow stark wild with rage: 'Sir, said not you,
You'd somewhat to discourse, not long ago,

With me in private?' 'I remember't well:
Some other time be sure, I will not fail:
Now I am in great haste upon my word:
A messenger came for me from a lord,
That's in a bad condition, like to die.'
'Oh! sir, he can't be in a worse than I:
Therefore for God's sake do not stir from hence.'
'Sweet sir! your pardon: 'tis of consequence:
I hope you're kinder than to press my stay,
Which may be Heav'n knows what out of my way.'
This said, he left me to my murderer.
Seeing no hopes of my relief appear,
'Confounded be the stars,' said I, 'that swayed
This fatal day! would I had kept my bed
With sickness, rather than been visited
With this worse plague! what ill have I e'er done,
To pull this curse, this heavy judgment down?'
    While I was thus lamenting my ill hap,
Comes aid at length: a brace of bailiffs clap
The rascal on the back: 'Here take your fees,
Kind gentlemen,' said I, 'for my release.'
He would have had me bail. 'Excuse me, sir,
I've made a vow ne'er to be surety more:
My father was undone by't heretofore.'
Thus I got off, and blessed the fates that he
Was pris'ner made, I set at liberty.

[June 1681]

The third satyr of Juvenal, imitated
*The poet brings in a friend of his, giving him an account
why he removes from London to live in the country.*

Though much concerned to leave my dear old friend,
I must however his design commend
Of fixing in the country: for were I
As free to choose my residence as he,
The Peak, the Fens, the Hundreds, or Land's-end,
I would prefer to Fleet-street, or the Strand.
What place so desert, and so wild is there,
Whose inconveniences one would not bear,
Rather than the alarms of midnight fire,
The fall of houses, knavery of cits,
The plots of factions, and the noise of wits,
And thousand other plagues, which up and down
Each day and hour infest the cursed town?
    As fate would have it, on the appointed day
Of parting hence, I met him on the way,
Hard by Mile-end, the place so famed of late,
In prose, and verse, for the great faction's treat;
Here we stood still, and after compliments
Of course, and wishing his good journey hence,
I asked what sudden causes made him fly
The once loved town, and his dear company:
When, on the hated prospect looking back,
Thus with just rage the good old Timon spake.
    'Since virtue here in no repute is had,
Since worth is scorned, learning and sense unpaid,
And knavery the only thriving trade;
Finding my slender fortune every day
Dwindle, and waste insensibly away,
I, like a losing gamester, thus retreat,
To manage wiselier my last stake of fate;
While I have strength, and want no staff to prop
My tott'ring limbs, ere age has made me stoop
Beneath its weight, ere all my thread be spun,
And life has yet in store some sands to run,
'Tis my resolve to quit the nauseous town.
    'Let thriving Morecraft choose his dwelling there,
Rich with the spoils of some young spendthrift heir:
Let the plot-mongers stay behind, whose art
Can truth to sham, and sham to truth convert:

Whoever has an house to build, or set,
His wife, his conscience, or his oath to let:
Whoever has, or hopes for offices,
A navy, guard, or custom-house's place:
Let sharping courtiers stay, who there are great
By putting the false dice on king and state:
Where they, who once were grooms, and footboys known,
Are now to fair estates, and honours grown;
Nor need we envy them, or wonder much
At their fantastic greatness, since they're such,
Whom fortune oft in her capricious freaks
Is pleased to raise from kennels, and the jakes,
To wealth, and dignity above the rest,
When she is frolic, and disposed to jest.
   'I live in London? What should I do there?
I cannot lie, nor flatter, nor forswear:
I can't commend a book, or piece of wit
(Though a lord were the author) dully writ:
I'm no Sir Sidrophel to read the stars,
And cast nativities for longing heirs,
When fathers shall drop off: no Gadbury
To tell the minute when the King shall die,
And you know what—come in: nor can I steer,
And tack about my conscience, whensoe'er
To a new point, I see religion veer.
Let others pimp to courtier's lechery,
I'll draw no city cuckold's curse on me:
Nor would I do it, though to be made great,
And raised to be chief Minister of State.
Therefore I think it fit to rid the town
Of one that is an useless member grown.
   'Besides, who has pretence to favour now,
But he, who hidden villainy does know,
Whose breast does with some burning secret glow?
By none thou shalt preferred, or valued be,
That trusts thee with an honest secrecy:
He only may to great men's friendship reach,
Who great men, when he pleases, can impeach.
Let others thus aspire to dignity;
For me, I'd not their envied grandeur buy
For all the Exchange is worth, that Paul's will cost,
Or was of late in the Scotch voyage lost.
What would it boot, if I, to gain my end,
Forego my quiet, and my ease of mind,
Still feared, at last betrayed by my great friend?

'Another cause, which I must boldly own,
And not the least, for which I quit the town,
Is to behold it made the common-shore
Where France does all her filth and ordure pour:
What spark of true old English rage can bear
Those, who were slaves at home, to lord it here?
We've all our fashions, language, compliments,
Our music, dances, curing, cooking thence;
And we shall have their poisoning too ere long,
If still in the improvement we go on.
What wouldst thou say, great Harry, shouldst thou view
Thy gaudy fluttering race of English now,
Their tawdry clothes, pulvilios, essences,
Their Chedreux perruques, and those vanities,
Which thou, and they of old did so despise?
What wouldst thou say to see th'infected town
With the foul spawn of foreigners o'errun?
Hither from Paris, and all parts they come,
The spew, and vomit of their gaols at home:
To court they flock, and to St James his Square,
And wriggle into great men's service there:
Footboys at first, till they, from wiping shoes,
Grow by degrees the masters of the house:
Ready of wit, hardened of impudence,
Able with ease to put down either Haines,
Both the King's player, and King's evidence;
Flippant of talk, and voluble of tongue,
With words at will, no lawyer better hung:
Softer than flattering court-parasite,
Or city trader, when he means to cheat,
No calling or profession comes amiss:
A needy monsieur can be what he please,
Groom, page, valet, quack, operator, fencer,
Perfumer, pimp, jack-pudding, juggler, dancer:
Give but the word, the cur will fetch and bring,
Come over to the Emperor, or King:
Or, if you please, fly o'er the pyramid,
Which Jordan and the rest in vain have tried.
      'Can I have patience, and endure to see
The paltry foreign wretch take place of me,
Whom the same wind and vessel brought ashore,
That brought prohibited goods, and dildoes o'er?
Then, pray, what mighty privilege is there
For me, that at my birth drew English air?
And where's the benefit to have my veins

Run British blood, if there's no difference
'Twixt me and him, the statute freedom gave,
And made a subject of a true-born slave?
'But nothing shocks, and is more loathed by me,
Than the vile rascal's fulsome flattery:
By help of this false magnifying glass,
A louse or flea shall for a camel pass:
Produce an hideous wight, more ugly far
Than those ill shapes which in old hangings are,
He'll make him straight a beau garçon appear:
Commend his voice and singing, though he bray
Worse than Sir Martin Marr-all in the play:
And, if he rhyme, shall praise for standard wit,
More scurvy sense than Prynne, and Vicars writ.
'And here's the mischief, though we say the same,
He is believed, and we are thought to sham:
Do you but smile, immediately the beast
Laughs out aloud, though he ne'er heard the jest:
Pretend you're sad, he's presently in tears,
Yet grieves no more than marble, when it wears
Sorrow in metaphor: but speak of heat,
'O God! how sultry 'tis!' he'll cry, and sweat
In depth of winter: straight, if you complain
Of cold, the weather-glass is sunk again:
Then he'll call for his frieze campaign, and swear
'Tis beyond eighty, he's in Greenland here.
Thus he shifts scenes, and oft'ner in a day
Can change his face, than actors at a play:
There's nought so mean can 'scape the flatt'ring sot,
Not his Lord's snuff-box, nor his powder-spot:
If he but spit, or pick his teeth, he'll cry,
'How everything becomes you! let me die,
Your lordship does it most judiciously!'
And swear 'tis fashionable if he sneeze,
Extremely taking, and it needs must please.
'Besides, there's nothing sacred, nothing free
From the hot satyr's rampant lechery:
Nor wife, nor virgin-daughter can escape,
Scarce thou thyself, or son avoid a rape:
All must go padlocked: if nought else there be,
Suspect thy very stables' chastity.
By this the vermin into secrets creep,
Thus families in awe they strive to keep.
What living for an Englishman is there,
Where such as these get head, and domineer,

Whose use and custom 'tis, never to share
A friend, but love to reign without dispute,
Without a rival, full and absolute?
Soon as the insect gets his Honour's ear,
And flyblows some of's pois'nous malice there,
Straight I'm turned off, kicked out of doors, discarded,
And all my former service disregarded.
   'But leaving these messieurs, for fear that I
Be thought of the silk-weaver's mutiny,
From the loathed subject let us hasten on,
To mention other grievances in town:
And further, what respect at all is had
Of poor men here? and how's their service paid,
Though they be ne'er so diligent to wait,
To sneak, and dance attendance on the great?
No mark of favour is to be obtained
By one that sues, and brings an empty hand;
And all his merit is but made a sport,
Unless he glut some cormorant at Court.
   ' 'Tis now a common thing, and usual here,
To see the son of some rich usurer
Take place of nobles, keep his first-rate whore,
And, for a vaulting bout or two, give more
Than a guard-captain's pay: meanwhile the breed
Of peers, reduced to poverty, and need,
Are fain to trudge to the Bankside, and there
Take up with porters' leavings, suburb ware,
There spend that blood, which their great ancestor
So nobly shed at Cressy heretofore,
At brothel-fights in some foul common-shore.
   'Produce an evidence, though just he be,
As righteous Job, or Abraham, or he
Whom Heaven, when whole nature shipwrecked was,
Thought worth the saving, of all human race;
Or t'other, who the flaming deluge 'scaped,
When Sodom's lechers angels would have raped:
How rich he is, must the first question be,
Next for his manners and integrity:
They'll ask, what equipage he keeps, and what
He's reckoned worth in money and estate,
For shrieve how oft he has been known to fine,
And with how many dishes he does dine.
For look what cash a person has in store,
Just so much credit has he, and no more:

Should I upon a thousand Bibles swear,
And call each Saint throughout the calendar,
To vouch my oath, it won't be taken here;
The poor slight Heav'n, and thunderbolts, they think,
And Heav'n itself does at such trifles wink.
'Besides, what store of gibing scoffs are thrown
On one that's poor, and meanly clad in town;
If his apparel seem but overworn,
His stocking out at heel, or breeches torn:
One takes occasion his ripped shoe to flout,
And swears't has been at prison-grates hung out;
Another shrewdly jeers his coarse cravat,
Because himself wears point, a third his hat,
And most unmercifully shows his wit,
If it be old, or does not cock aright.
Nothing in poverty so ill is borne,
As its exposing men to grinning scorn,
To be by tawdry coxcombs pissed upon
And made the jesting stock of each buffoon.
'Turn out there, friend!' cries one at church, 'the pew
Is not for such mean scoundrel curs as you:
'Tis for your betters kept:' belike some sot
That knew no father, was on bulks begot,
But now is raised to an estate and pride,
By having the kind proverb on his side:
Let Gripe and Cheatwell take their places there,
And Dash, the scrivener's gaudy sparkish heir,
That wears three ruined orphans on his back:
Meanwhile, you in the alley stand, and sneak:
And you therewith must rest contented, since
Almighty wealth does put such difference.
What citizen a son-in-law will take,
Bred ne'er so well, that can't a jointure make?
What man of sense, that's poor, e'er summoned is
Amongst the Common Council to advise?
At vestry-consults when does he appear,
For choosing of some parish officer,
Or making leather buckets for the choir?
  ' 'Tis hard for any man to rise, that feels
His virtue clogged with poverty at heels;
But harder 'tis by much in London, where
A sorry lodging, coarse, and slender fare,
Fire, water, breathing, everything is dear:
Yet such as these an earthen dish disdain,
With which their ancestors, in Edgar's reign,

Were served, and thought it no disgrace to dine,
Though they were rich, had store of leather coin.
Low as their fortune is, yet they despise
A man that walks the streets in homely frieze:
To speak the truth, great part of England now,
In their own cloth will scarce vouchsafe to go:
Only, the statute's penalty to save,
Some few perhaps wear woollen in the grave.
Here all go daily dressed, although it be
Above their means, their rank, and quality:
The most in borrowed gallantry are clad,
For which the tradesmen's books are still unpaid:
This fault is common in the meaner sort,
That they must needs affect to bear the port
Of gentlemen, though they want income for't.
   'Sir, to be short, in this expensive town
There's nothing without money to be done:
What will you give to be admitted there,
And brought to speech of some Court Minister?
What will you give to have the quarter-face,
The squint and nodding go-by of his Grace?
His porter, groom, and steward must have fees,
And you may see the Tombs, and Tower for less:
Hard fate of suitors! who must pay, and pray
To livery-slaves, yet oft go scorned away.
   'Whoe'er at Barnet, or St Albans fears
To have his lodging drop about his ears,
Unless a sudden hurricane befall,
Or such a wind as blew old Noll to Hell?
Here, we build slight, what scarce outlasts the lease,
Without the help of props and buttresses:
And houses now-a-days as much require
To be ensured from falling, as from fire.
There, buildings are substantial, though less neat,
And kept with care both wind, and water tight:
There, you in safe security are blessed,
And nought, but conscience, to disturb your rest.
   'I am for living where no fires affright,
No bells rung backward break my sleep at night:
I scarce lie down, and draw my curtains here,
But straight I'm roused by the next house on fire:
Pale, and half dead with fear, myself I raise,
And find my room all over in a blaze;
By this't has seized on the third stairs, and I

E

Can now discern no other remedy,
But leaping out at window to get free :
For if the mischief from the cellar came,
Be sure the garret is the last takes flame.
'The moveables of Pordage were a bed
For him and's wife, a piss-pot by its side,
A looking-glass upon the cupboard's head,
A comb-case, candlestick, and pewter spoon,
For want of plate, with desk to write upon :
A box without a lid served to contain
Few authors, which made up his Vatican :
And there his own immortal works were laid,
On which the barbarous mice for hunger preyed.
Pordage had nothing, all the world does know,
And yet should he have lost this nothing too,
No one the wretched bard would have supplied
With lodging, house-room, or a crust of bread.
   'But if the fire burn down some great man's house,
All straight are interested in the loss :
The Court is straight in mourning sure enough,
The act, commencement, and the term put off :
Then we mischances of the town lament,
And fasts are kept, like judgments to prevent.
Out comes a brief immediately, with speed
To gather charity as far as Tweed.
Nay, while 'tis burning, some will send him in
Timber, and stone to build his house again :
Others choice furniture : here some rare piece
Of Rubens, or Vandyke presented is,
There a rich suit of Mortlack tapestry,
A bed of damask or embroidery :
One gives a fine scrutoire, or cabinet,
Another a huge massy dish of plate,
Or bag of gold : thus he at length gets more
By kind misfortune than he had before :
And all suspect it for a laid design,
As if he did himself the fire begin.
Could you but be advised to leave the town,
And from dear plays, and drinking friends be drawn,
A handsome dwelling might be had in Kent,
Surrey, or Essex, at a cheaper rent
Than what you're forced to give for one half year
To lie, like lumber, in a garret here :
A garden there, and well, that needs no rope,
Engine, or pains to crane its waters up :

Water is there through Nature's pipes conveyed,
For which no custom, or excise is paid.
Had I the smallest spot of ground, which scarce
Would summer half a dozen grasshoppers,
Not larger than my grave, though hence remote,
Far as St Michael's Mount, I would go to't,
Dwell there content, and thank the Fates to boot.
 'Here want of rest a-nights more people kills
Than all the college, and the weekly bills:
Where none have privilege to sleep, but those
Whose purses can compound for their respose:
In vain I go to bed, or close my eyes,
Methinks the place the middle region is,
Where I lie down in storms, in thunder rise:
The restless bells such din in steeples keep,
That scarce the dead can in their churchyards sleep:
Huzzas of drunkards, bellmen's midnight rhymes,
The noise of shops, with hawkers' early screams,
Besides the brawls of coachmen, when they meet,
And stop in turnings of a narrow street,
Such a loud medley of confusion make,
As drowsy Archer on the Bench would wake.
 'If you walk out in business ne'er so great,
Ten thousand stops you must expect to meet:
Thick crowds in every place you must charge through,
And storm your passage wheresoe'er you go:
While tides of followers behind you throng,
And, pressing on your heels, shove you along:
One with a board, or rafter, hits your head,
Another with his elbow bores your side;
Some tread upon your corns, perhaps in sport,
Meanwhile your legs are cased all o'er with dirt.
Here, you the march of a slow funeral wait,
Advancing to the church with solemn state:
There, a sedan, and lacquies stop your way,
That bears some punk of honour to the play:
Now, you some mighty piece of timber meet,
Which tott'ring threatens ruin to the street:
Next, a huge Portland stone, for building Paul's,
Itself almost a rock, on carriage rolls;
Which, if it fall, would cause a massacre,
And serve at once to murder, and inter.
 'If what I've said can't from the town affright,
Consider other dangers of the night:
When brickbats are from upper stories thrown,

And empty chamber-pots come pouring down
From garret windows: you have cause to bless
The gentle stars, if you come off with piss:
So many fates attend, a man had need
Ne'er walk without a surgeon by his side,
And he can hardly now discreet be thought,
That does not make his will ere he go out.
   'If this you 'scape, twenty to one you meet
Some of the drunken scourers of the street,
Flushed with success of warlike deeds performed,
Of constables subdued, and brothels stormed:
These, if a quarrel or a fray be missed,
Are ill at ease a-nights, and want their rest:
For mischief is a lechery to some,
And serves to make them sleep like laudanum.
Yet heated, as they are, with youth, and wine,
If they discern a train of flambeaux shine,
If a great man with his gilt coach appear,
And a strong guard of footboys in the rear,
The rascals sneak, and shrink their heads for fear.
Poor me, who use no light to walk about,
Save what the parish, or the skies hang out,
They value not: 'tis worth your while to hear
The scuffle, if that be a scuffle, where
Another gives the blows, I only bear:
He bids me stand: of force I must give way,
For 'twere a senseless thing to disobey,
And struggle here, where I'd as good oppose
Myself to Pembroke and his mastiffs loose.
'Who's there?' he cries, and takes you by the throat;
'Dog! are you dumb? Speak quickly, else my foot
Shall march about your buttocks: whence d'ye come?
From what bulk-ridden strumpet reeking home?
Saving your reverend pimpship, where d'ye ply?
How may one have a job of lechery?'
If you say anything, or hold your peace,
And silently go off, 'tis all a case:
Still he lays on: nay well, if you 'scape so:
Perhaps he'll clap an action on you too
Of battery, nor need he fear to meet
A jury to his turn, shall do him right,
And bring him in large damage for a shoe
Worn out, besides the pains, in kicking you.
A poor man must expect nought of redress,
But patience: his best way in such a case

Is to be thankful for the drubs, and beg
That they would mercifully spare one leg,
Or arm unbroke, and let him go away
With teeth enough to eat his meat next day.
   'Nor is this all which you have cause to fear:
Oft we encounter midnight padders here,
When the exchanges, and the shops are close,
And the rich tradesman in his counting-house
To view the profits of the day withdraws.
Hither in flocks from Shooter's Hill they come,
To seek their prize and booty nearer home:
'Your purse!' they cry; 'tis madness to resist,
Or strive, with a cocked pistol at your breast:
And these each day so strong and numerous grow,
The town can scarce afford them jail-room now.
Happy the times of the old Heptarchy,
Ere London knew so much of villainy:
Then fatal carts through Holborn seldom went,
And Tyburn with few pilgrims was content:
A less, and single prison then would do,
And served the City and the County too.
   'These are the reasons, sir, which drive me hence,
To which I might add more, would time dispense
To hold you longer; but the sun draws low,
The coach is hard at hand, and I must go:
Therefore, dear sir, farewell; and when the town
From better company can spare you down,
To make the country with your presence blessed,
Then visit your old friend amongst the rest:
There I'll find leisure to unlade my mind
Of what remarks I now must leave behind,
The fruits of dear experience, which, with these
Improved, will serve for hints, and notices;
And when you write again, may be of use
To furnish satyr for your daring muse.'

[May 1682]

A satyr, addressed to a friend
that is about to leave the University,
and come abroad in the world

If you're so out of love with happiness,
To quit a college life, and learned ease,
Convince me first, and some good reasons give,
What methods and designs you'll take to live:
For such resolves are needful in the case,
Before you tread the world's mysterious maze:
Without the premises, in vain you'll try
To live by systems of philosophy:
Your Aristotle, Cartes, and Le Grand,
And Euclid too, in little stead will stand.
  How many men of choice, and noted parts,
Well fraught with learning, languages, and arts,
Designing high preferment in their mind,
And little doubting good success to find,
With vast and tow'ring thoughts have flocked to town,
But to their cost soon found themselves undone,
Now to repent, and starve at leisure left,
Of misery's last comfort, hope, bereft!
  'These failed for want of good advice,' you cry,
'Because at first they fixed on no employ:'
Well then, let's draw the prospect, and the scene
To all the advantage possibly we can:
The world lies now before you, let me hear
What course your judgment counsels you to steer:
Always considered, that your whole estate,
And all your fortune lies beneath your hat:
Were you the son of some rich usurer,
That starved, and damned himself to make his heir,
Left nought to do, but to inter the sot,
And spend with ease what he with pains had got;
'Twere easy to advise how you might live,
Nor would there need instruction then to give:
But you, that boast of no inheritance,
Save that small stock which lies within your brains,
Learning must be your trade, and therefore weigh
With heed how you your game the best may play;
Bethink yourself awhile, and then propose
What way of life is fitt'st for you to choose.

If you for orders, and a gown design,
Consider only this, dear friend of mine,
The church is grown so overstocked of late,
That if you walk abroad, you'll hardly meet
More porters now than parsons in the street.
At every corner they are forced to ply
For jobs of hawkering divinity:
And half the number of the sacred herd
Are fain to stroll, and wander unpreferred.
　If this, or thoughts of such a weighty charge,
Make you resolve to keep yourself at large,
For want of better opportunity,
A school must your next sanctuary be:
Go, wed some grammar-bridewell, and a wife,
And there beat Greek, and Latin for your life:
With birchen sceptre there command at will,
Greater than Busby's self, or Doctor Gill:
But who would be to the vile drudg'ry bound
Where there so small encouragement is found?
Where you for recompense of all your pains
Shall hardly reach a common fiddler's gains?
For when you've toiled, and laboured all you can,
To dung, and cultivate a barren brain,
A dancing master shall be better paid,
Though he instructs the heels, and you the head:
To such indulgence are kind parents grown,
That nought costs less in breeding than a son:
Nor is it hard to find a father now,
Shall more upon a setting-dog allow,
And with a freer hand reward the care
Of training up his spaniel, than his heir.
　Some think themselves exalted to the sky,
If they light in some noble family:
Diet, an horse, and thirty pounds a year,
Besides th'advantage of his Lordship's ear,
The credit of the business, and the state,
Are things that in a youngster's sense sound great.
Little the inexperienced wretch does know,
What slavery he oft must undergo,
Who, though in silken scarf, and cassock dressed,
Wears but a gayer livery at best:
When dinner calls, the implement must wait
With holy words to consecrate the meat,
But hold it for a favour seldom known,
If he be deigned the honour to sit down:

Soon as the tarts appear, Sir Crape, withdraw!
Those dainties are not for a spiritual maw:
Observe your distance, and be sure to stand
Hard by the cistern with your cap in hand:
There for diversion you may pick your teeth,
Till the kind voider comes for your relief:
For mere board wages such their freedom sell,
Slaves to an hour, and vassals to a bell:
And if th'enjoyment of one day be stole,
They are but pris'ners out upon parole:
Always the marks of slavery remain,
And they, though loose, still drag about their chain.
  And where's the mighty prospect after all,
A chaplainship served up, and seven years' thrall?
The menial thing, perhaps, for a reward,
Is to some slender benefice preferred,
With this proviso bound, that he must wed
My lady's antiquated waiting-maid,
In dressing only skilled, and marmalade.
  Let others, who such meannesses can brook,
Strike countenance to every great man's look:
Let those that have a mind, turn slaves to eat,
And live contented by another's plate:
I rate my freedom higher, nor will I
For food and raiment truck my liberty.
But, if I must to my last shifts be put,
To fill a bladder, and twelve yards of gut,
Rather with counterfeited wooden leg,
And my right arm tied up, I'll choose to beg:
I'll rather choose to starve at large, than be
The gaudiest vassal to dependency.
  'T has ever been the top of my desires,
The utmost height to which my wish aspires,
That Heav'n would bless me with a small estate,
Where I might find a close obscure retreat;
There, free from noise, and all ambitious ends,
Enjoy a few choice books, and fewer friends,
Lord of myself, accountable to none,
But to my conscience, and my God alone:
There live unthought of, and unheard of die,
And grudge mankind my very memory.
But since the blessing is, I find, too great
For me to wish for, or expect of fate;
Yet, maugre all the spite of destiny,
My thoughts and actions are, and shall be, free.

A certain author, very grave, and sage,
This story tells: no matter what the page.
One time, as they walked forth ere break of day,
The wolf and dog encountered on the way:
Famished the one, meagre, and lean of plight,
As a cast poet, who for bread does write:
The other fat, and plump, as prebend was,
Pampered with luxury and holy ease.
    Thus met, with compliments, too long to tell,
Of being glad to see each other well:
'How now, Sir Towzer?' said the wolf, 'I pray,
Whence comes it that you look so sleek and gay?
While I, who do as well, I am sure, deserve,
For want of livelihood am like to starve?'
    'Troth, sir,' replied the dog, ' 't has been my fate,
I thank the friendly stars, to hap of late
On a kind master, to whose care I owe
All this good flesh, wherewith you see me now:
From his rich voider every day I'm fed
With bones of fowls, and crusts of finest bread:
With fricassee, ragout, and whatso'er
Of costly kickshaws now in fashion are,
And more variety of boiled and roast,
Than a Lord Mayor's waiter e'er could boast.
Then, sir, 'tis hardly credible to tell,
How I'm respected, and beloved by all:
I'm the delight of the whole family,
Not darling Shock more favourite than I:
I never sleep abroad, to air exposed,
But in my warm apartment am inclosed:
There on fresh bed of straw, with canopy
Of hutch above, like dog of state I lie.
Besides, when with high fare and nature fired,
To generous sports of youth I am inspired,
All the proud shes are soft to my embrace,
From bitch of quality down to turnspit race:
Each day I try new mistresses and loves,
Nor envy sovereign dogs in their alcoves.
Thus happy I of all enjoy the best,
No mortal cur on earth yet half so blessed;
And farther to enhance the happiness,
All this I get by idleness, and ease.'
    'Troth,' said the wolf, 'I envy your estate:
Would to the gods it were but my good fate,

F

That I might happily admitted be
A member of your blessed society!
I would with faithfulness discharge my place
In any thing that I might serve his Grace:
But, think you, sir, it would be feasible,
And that my application might prevail?'
    'Do but endeavour, sir, you need not doubt;
I make no question but to bring't about:
Only rely on me, and rest secure,
I'll serve you to the utmost of my power,
As I am a dog of honour, sir: —but this
I only take the freedom to advise,
That you'd a little lay your roughness by,
And learn to practise complaisance like me.'
    'For that let me alone: I'll have a care,
And top my part, I warrant, to a hair:
There's not a courtier of them all shall vie
For fawning, and for suppleness with me.'
    And thus resolved at last, the travellers
Towards the house together shape their course:
The dog, who breeding well did understand,
In walking gives his guest the upper hand:
And as they walk along, they all the while
With mirth and pleasant raillery beguile
The tedious time and way, till day drew near,
And light came on; by which did soon appear
The mastiff's neck to view, all worn and bare.
    This when his comrade spied, 'What means,' said he,
'This circle bare, which round your neck I see?
If I may be so bold;' – 'Sir, you must know,
That I at first was rough, and fierce, like you,
Of nature cursed, and often apt to bite
Strangers, and else, whoever came in sight:
For this I was tied up, and underwent
The whip sometimes, and such light chastisement;
Till I at length by discipline grew tame,
Gentle, and tractable, as now I am:
'Twas by this short, and slight severity
I gained these marks and badges which you see:
But what are they? Allons, monsieur! let's go.'
'Not one step farther: Sir, excuse me now.
Much joy t'ye of your envied, blessed estate.
I will not buy preferment at that rate:

A God's name, take your golden chains for me:
Faith, I'd not be a king, not to be free:
Sir dog, your humble servant, so Godbw'y.

[probably 1682]

A satyr concerning poetry
*The person of Spenser is brought in, dissuading the author from the
study of poetry, and showing how little it is esteemed and encouraged
in this present age.*

One night, as I was pondering of late
On all the mis'ries of my hapless fate,
Cursing my rhyming stars, raving in vain
At all the powers which over poets reign,
In came a ghastly shape, all pale and thin,
As some poor sinner who by priest had been,
Under a long Lent's penance, starved and whipped,
Or parboiled lecher, late from hothouse crept :
Famished his looks appeared, his eyes sunk in,
Like morning-gown about him hung his skin,
A wreath of laurel on his head he wore,
A book, inscribed the *Fairy Queen*, he bore.
   By this I knew him, rose, and bowed, and said,
'Hail reverend ghost! all hail most sacred shade!
Why this great visit? why vouchsafed to me,
The meanest of thy British progeny?
Com'st thou in my uncalled, unhallowed muse,
Some of thy mighty spirit to infuse?
If so, lay on thy hands, ordain me fit
For the high cure and ministry of wit :
Let me, I beg, thy great instructions claim,
Teach me to tread the glorious paths of fame :
Teach me, for none does better know than thou,
How, like thyself, I may immortal grow.'
   Thus did I speak, and spoke it in a strain
Above my common rate and usual vein,
As if inspired by presence of the bard,
Who, with a frown, thus to reply was heard,
In style of satyr such wherein of old
He the famed tale of *Mother Hubbard* told.
   'I come, fond idiot, ere it be too late,
Kindly to warn thee of thy wretched fate :
Take heed betimes, repent, and learn of me
To shun the dang'rous rocks of poetry :
Had I the choice of flesh and blood again,
To act once more in life's tumultuous scene,
I'd be a porter, or a scavenger,
A groom, or anything, but poet here.

Hast thou observed some hawker of the town,
Who through the streets with dismal scream and tone,
Cries matches, small-coal, brooms, old shoes, and boots,
Socks, sermons, ballads, lies, gazettes, and votes?
So unrecorded to the grave I'd go,
And nothing but the register tell who:
Rather that poor unheard-of wretch I'd be,
Than the most glorious name in poetry,
With all its boasted immortality:
Rather than he, who sung on Phrygia's shore,
The Grecian bullies fighting for a whore:
Or he of Thebes, whom fame so much extols
For praising jockeys, and Newmarket fools.
    'So many now, and bad, the scribblers be,
'Tis scandal to be of the company:
The foul disease is so prevailing grown,
So much the fashion of the Court and town,
That scarce a man well-bred in either's deemed,
But who has killed, been often clapped, and oft has rhymed:
The fools are troubled with a flux of brains,
And each on paper squirts his filthy sense:
A leash of sonnets, and a dull lampoon
Set up an author, who forthwith is grown
A man of parts, of rhyming, and renown:
Ev'n that vile wretch, who in lewd verse each year
Describes the pageants, and my good Lord Mayor,
Whose works must serve the next election day
For making squibs, and under pies to lay,
Yet counts himself of the inspired train,
And dares in thought the sacred name profane.
    'But is it nought,' thou'lt say, 'in front to stand,
With laurel crowned by White, or Loggan's hand?
Is it not great, and glorious to be known,
Marked out, and gazed at through the wondering town,
By all the rabble passing up and down?'
So Oates and Bedloe have been pointed at,
And every busy coxcomb of the state:
The meanest felons who through Holborn go,
More eyes and looks than twenty poets draw:
If this be all, go, have thy posted name
Fixed up with bills of quack, and public sham,
To be the stop of gaping prentices,
And read by reeling drunkards, when they piss;
Or else to lie exposed on trading stall,

While the bilked owner hires gazettes to tell,
'Mongst spaniels lost, that author does not sell.
  'Perhaps, fond fool, thou sooth'st thyself in dream,
With hopes of purchasing a lasting name?
Thou think'st, perhaps, thy trifles shall remain,
Like sacred Cowley, or immortal Ben?
But who of all the bold adventurers,
Who now drive on the trade of fame in verse,
Can be ensured in this unfaithful sea,
Where there so many lost and shipwrecked be?
How many poems writ in ancient time,
Which thy forefathers had in great esteem,
Which in the crowded shops bore any rate,
And sold like news-books, and affairs of state,
Have grown contemptible, and slighted since,
As Pordage, Flecknoe, or the *British Prince*?
Quarles, Chapman, Heywood, Withers had applause,
And Wild, and Ogilby in former days;
But now are damned to wrapping drugs and wares,
And cursed by all their broken stationers:
And so may'st thou, perchance, pass up and down,
And please awhile th'admiring court and town,
Who after shalt in Duck-lane shops be thrown,
To mould with Silvester, and Shirley there,
And truck for pots of ale next Stourbridge fair.
Then who'll not laugh to see th'immortal name
To vile Mundungus made a martyr flame?
And all thy deathless monuments of wit,
Wipe porters' tails, or mount in paper kite?
  'But, grant thy poetry should find success,
And (which is rare) the squeamish critics please;
Admit it read, and praised, and courted be
By this nice age, and all posterity;
If thou expectest aught but empty fame,
Condemn thy hopes and labours to the flame:
The rich have now learned only to admire;
He, who to greater favours does aspire,
Is mercenary thought, and writes to hire:
Wouldst thou to raise thine, and thy country's fame,
Choose some old English hero for thy theme,
Bold Arthur, or great Edward's greater son,
Or our fifth Harry, matchless in renown;
Make Agincourt, and Cressy fields outvie
The famed Lavinian shores, and walls of Troy;

What Scipio, what Mæcenas wouldst thou find,
What Sidney now to thy great project kind?
'Bless me! how great his genius! how each line
Is big with sense! how glorious a design
Does through the whole, and each proportion shine!
How lofty all his thoughts, and how inspired!
Pity, such wondrous thoughts are not preferred,'
Cries a gay wealthy sot, who would not bail
For bare five pounds, the author out of jail,
Should he starve there, and rot; who, if a brief
Came out the needy poets to relieve,
To the whole tribe would scarce a tester give;
But fifty guineas for a whore and clap!
The peer's well used, and comes off wondrous cheap:
A poet would be dear, and out o' th' way,
Should he expect above a coachman's pay:
For this will any dedicate, and lie,
And daub the gaudy ass with flattery?
For this will any prostitute his sense
To coxcombs void of bounty, as of brains?
Yet such is the hard fate of writers now,
They're forced for alms to each great name to bow,
Fawn, like her lap-dog, on her tawdry Grace,
Commend her beauty, and belie her glass,
By which she every morning primes her face:
Sneak to his Honour, call him witty, brave,
And just, though a known coward, fool, or knave;
And praise his lineage and nobility,
Whose arms at first came from the Company.
    "'Tis so, 'twas ever so, since heretofore
The blind old bard, with dog and bell before,
Was fain to sing for bread from door to door:
The needy muses all turned gipsies then,
And of the begging trade e'er since have been:
Should mighty Sappho in these days revive,
And hope upon her stock of wit to live,
She must to Creswell's trudge to mend her gains,
And let her tail to hire, as well as brains.
What poet ever fined for sheriff? or who
By wit and sense did ever Lord Mayor grow?
    'My own hard usage here I need not press,
Where you have every day before your face
Plenty of fresh resembling instances:
Great Cowley's muse the same ill treatment had,

Whose verse shall live for ever to upbraid
Th'ungrateful world, that left such worth unpaid.
Waller himself may thank inheritance
For what he else had never got by sense.
On Butler who can think without just rage,
The glory, and the scandal of the age?
Fair stood his hopes, when first he came to town,
Met everywhere with welcomes of renown,
Courted, and loved by all, with wonder read,
And promises of princely favour fed:
But what reward for all had he at last,
After a life in dull expectance passed?
The wretch at summing up his misspent days
Found nothing left, but poverty, and praise:
Of all his gains by verse he could not save
Enough to purchase flannel and a grave:
Reduced to want, he in due time fell sick,
Was fain to die, and be interred on tick:
And well might bless the fever that was sent,
To rid him hence, and his worse fate prevent.
    'You've seen what fortune other poets share:
View next the factors of the theatre,
That constant mart, which all the year does hold,
Where staple wit is bartered, bought, and sold;
Here trading scribblers for their maintenance
And livelihood trust to a lottery-chance:
But who his parts would in the service spend,
Where all his hopes on vulgar breath depend?
Where every sot, for paying half-a-crown,
Has the prerogative to cry him down?
Sedley indeed may be content with fame,
Nor care should an ill-judging audience damn;
But Settle, and the rest, that write for pence,
Whose whole estate's an ounce or two of brains,
Should a thin house on the third day appear,
Must starve, or live in tatters all the year.
And what can we expect that's brave and great,
From a poor needy wretch, that writes to eat?
Who the success of the next play must wait
For lodging, food, and clothes, and whose chief care
Is how to spunge for the next meal, and where?
    'Hadst thou of old in flourishing Athens lived,
When all the learned arts in glory thrived,
When mighty Sophocles the stage did sway,
And poets by the state were held in pay;

'Twere worth thy pains to cultivate thy muse,
And daily wonders then it might produce;
But who would now write hackney to a stage,
That's only thought the nuisance of the age?
Go, after this, and beat thy wretched brains,
And toil to bring in thankless idiots' means:
Turn o'er dull Horace, and the classic fools,
To poach for sense, and hunt for idle rules:
Be free of tickets, and the playhouses,
To make some tawdry actress there thy prize,
And spend thy third day's gains 'twixt her clapped thighs.
  'All trades, and all professions here abound,
And yet encouragement for all is found:
Here a vile emp'ric, who by licence kills,
Who every week helps to increase the bills,
Wears velvet, keeps his coach, and whore beside,
For what less villains must to Tyburn ride.
There a dull trading sot, in wealth o'ergrown
By thriving knavery, can call his own
A dozen manors, and if fate still bless,
Expects as many counties to possess.
Punks, panders, bawds, all their due pensions gain,
And every day the great men's bounty drain;
Lavish expense on wit, has never yet
Been taxed amongst the grievances of state.
The Turkey, Guinea, India gainers be,
And all but the poetic company:
Each place of traffic, Bantam, Smyrna, Zante,
Greenland, Virginia, Seville, Alicant,
And France, that sends us dildoes, lace and wine,
Vast profit all, and large returns bring in:
Parnassus only is that barren coast,
Where the whole voyage, and adventure's lost.
  'Then be advised, the slighted muse forsake,
And Coke and Dalton for thy study take:
For fees each term sweat in the crowded hall,
And there for charters, and cracked titles bawl,
Where Maynard thrives, and pockets more each year
Than forty laureats of the theatre.
Or else to orders, and the church betake
Thyself, and that thy future refuge make:
There fawn on some proud patron to engage
Th'advowson of cast punk, and parsonage:
Or soothe the Court, and preach up kingly right,
To gain a prebend or a mitre by't.

In fine, turn pettifogger, canonist,
Civilian, pedant, mountebank, or priest,
Soldier, or merchant, fiddler, painter, fencer,
Jack-pudding, juggler, player, or rope-dancer:
Preach, plead, cure, fight, game, pimp, beg, cheat, or thieve;
Be all but poet, and there's way to live.
   'But why do I in vain my counsel spend
On one whom there's so little hope to mend?
Where I perhaps as fruitlessly exhort,
As Lenten doctors, when they preach at court;
Not entered punks from lust they once have tried,
Not fops, and women from conceit and pride,
Not bawds from impudence, cowards from fear,
Nor seared unfeeling sinners past despair,
Are half so hard and stubborn to reduce,
As a poor wretch when once possessed with muse.
   'If, therefore, what I've said cannot avail,
Nor from the rhyming folly thee recall,
But spite of all thou wilt be obstinate,
And run thyself upon avoidless fate;
Mayst thou go on unpitied, till thou be
Brought to the parish, bridge, and beggary;
Till urged by want, like broken scribblers, thou
Turn poet to a booth, a Smithfield show,
And write heroic verse for Barthol'mew:
   Then slighted by the very Nursery,
   May'st thou at last be forced to starve, like me.'

[probably 1682]

Catullus. Epigram VII, imitated

Nay, Lesbia, never ask me this,
How many kisses will suffice?
Faith, 'tis a question hard to tell,
Exceeding hard; for you as well
May ask what sums of gold suffice
The greedy miser's boundless wish:
Think what drops the ocean store,
With all the sands that make its shore:
Think what spangles deck the skies,
When Heaven looks with all its eyes:
Or think how many atoms came
To compose this mighty frame:
Let all these the counters be,
To tell how oft I'm kissed by thee:
Till no malicious spy can guess
To what vast height the scores arise;
Till weak arithmetic grow scant,
And numbers for the reck'ning want:
All these will hardly be enough
For me stark staring mad with love.

[probably 1682]

A fragment of Petronius, paraphrased

I hate fruition, now 'tis past:
'Tis all but nastiness at best,
The homeliest thing that man can do;
Besides, 'tis short, and fleeting, too:
A squirt of slippery delight
That with a moment takes its flight,
A fulsome bliss that soon does cloy,
And make us loathe what we enjoy.
Then let us not too eager run,
By passion blindly hurried on,
Like beasts, who nothing better know
Than what mere lust incites them to:
For when in floods of love we're drenched,
The flames are by enjoyment quenched:
But thus, let's thus together lie,
And kiss out long eternity:
Here we dread no conscious spies,
No blushes stain our guiltless joys;
Here no faintness dulls desires,
And pleasure never flags, nor tires:
This has pleased, and pleases now,
And for ages will do so.
   Enjoyment here is never done,
But fresh, and always but begun.

[probably 1682]

An allusion to Martial
Book I: epigram CXVIII

As oft, Sir Tradewel, as we meet,
You're sure to ask me in the street,
When you shall send your boy to me
To fetch my book of poetry,
And promise you'll but read it o'er,
And faithfully the loan restore:
But let me tell ye as a friend,
You need not take the pains to send:
'Tis a long way to where I dwell,
At farther end of Clerkenwell:
There in a garret near the sky,
Above five pair of stairs I lie.
But, if you'd have what you pretend,
You may procure it nearer hand:
In Cornhill, where you often go,
Hard by th'Exchange, there is, you know,
A shop of rhyme, where you may see
The posts all clad in poetry;
There Hindmarsh lives, of high renown,
The noted'st Tory in the town,
Where, if you please, enquire for me,
And he, or's prentice, presently
From the next shelf will reach you down
The piece well bound for half-a-crown:
'The price is much too dear,' you cry,
'To give for both the book, and me:'
Yes, doubtless, for such vanities,
We know, Sir, you are too, too wise.

[probably 1682]

An ode of Anacreon, paraphrased

Make me a bowl, a mighty bowl,
Large, as my capacious soul,
Vast, as my thirst is; let it have
Depth enough to be my grave –
I mean the grave of all my care,
For I intend to bury't there.
Let it of silver fashioned be,
Worthy of wine, worthy of me,
Worthy to adorn the spheres,
As that bright cup amongst the stars,
That cup which Heaven deigned a place
Next the sun, its greatest grace.
Kind cup! that to the stars did go,
To light poor drunkards here below:
Let mine be so, and give me light,
That I may drink, and revel by't;
Yet draw no shapes of armour there,
No cask, nor shield, nor sword, not spear,
Nor wars of Thebes, not wars of Troy,
Nor any other martial toy:
For what do I vain armour prize,
Who mind not such rough exercise,
But gentler sieges, softer wars,
Fights that cause no wounds or scars?
I'll have no battles on my plate,
Lest sight of them should brawls create,
Lest that provoke to quarrels too,
Which wine itself enough can do.
Draw me no constellations there,
No Ram, nor Bull, nor Dog, nor Bear.
Nor any of that monstrous fry
Of animals which stock the sky:
For what are stars to my design,
Stars, which I, when drunk, outshine,
Outshone by every drop of wine?
I lack no Pole-star on the brink
To guide in the wide sea of drink,
But would for ever there be tossed;
And wish no haven, seek no coast.
Yet, gentle artist, if thou'lt try
Thy skill, then draw me (let me see)

Draw me first a spreading vine,
Make its arms the bowl entwine
With kind embraces, such as I
Twist about my loving she;
Let its boughs o'erspread above
Scenes of drinking, scenes of love.
Draw next the patron of that tree,
Draw Bacchus, and soft Cupid by;
Draw them both in toping shapes,
Their temples crowned with clustered grapes:
Make them lean against the cup,
As 'twere to keep their figures up;
And when their reeling forms I view,
I'll think them drunk, and be so too:
  The Gods shall my examples be,
  The Gods, thus drunk in effigy.

[probably 1682]